PRAISE FOR
GLIMPSES OF ANOTHER WORLD

Glimpses of Another World is more than a book about Instrumental Trans Communication (ITC), allegedly the method that through electronic devices may establish a bridge with another dimension beyond death. This book is the story of a woman, a career diplomat, who renounced her professional and personal life to devote herself entirely to the quest of finding out if there could be a continuity of consciousness beyond this life. She writes that the bridge with the next world is only attained when the heart and the soul strive for it: love is the unassailable force behind positive results that convinced her of the reality of survival. It is indeed a fascinating journey in which she engaged herself.

~ **Pim van Lommel, cardiologist, NDE-researcher, author of** *Consciousness beyond Life.*

Glimpses of Another World is absolutely unique. Several investigators, Anabela Cardoso among them, have described their efforts to communicate with deceased persons using electronic devices. However, this book describes Cardoso's quest in very personal terms, describing the way that life events launched these efforts and the manner in which the results impacted both her worldview and her personal life. Readers will be intrigued by Cardoso's observations on mediumship, free will, cause-and-effect, and the possibility that animals survive death. A lengthy appendix provides readers with instructions on how they attempt communication themselves, joining the cadre of bold explorers who are trying to understand what is certainly the greatest unsolved mystery of our time.

~ **Stanley Krippner, Ph.D., Affiliated Distinguished Professor, California Institute of Integral Studies.**
Co-author, *Personal Mythology* and co-editor
Varieties of Anomalous Experience:
Examining the Scientific Evidence.

GLIMPSES
OF ANOTHER
WORLD

GLIMPSES
OF ANOTHER
WORLD

Impressions and Reflections
of an EVP Operator

ANABELA CARDOSO

www.whitecrowbooks.com

A NOTE ON THE COVER

On December 15, 2018 at 00.42h, I went to Rio do Tempo's room in my house to say my night prayers (or silent thoughts) as I do every day. The light was off as it always is and I was sitting on the floor in front of the window as usual.

The moment I started speaking mentally to my beloved communicators, a strong flash of light like a blue ball, or a blue star, hit the glass of the window with a big bang. I was stunned and for a moment it scared me. I thought the window would break but it didn't. Perhaps it hit the wood that separates both glass panels, I can't say for sure. I clearly saw this incredible light ball with points in the shape of a big star (for lack of a better image but the centre was round and the colour electric or petrol blue).

It occurred to me that it might have been an electric problem of some kind and that the electricity in the house might be off although there had been no storms that day.

I got up and I checked the lights in and outside the house and all were working normally.

I didn't know what to think. I was alone at the time and started shaking but tried to recover and went back into the room, my ITC studio that I love.

I sat down again and spoke mentally to Rio do Tempo as I do many times, still shaking; They said, also mentally, "It was us, it's always us". Other occurrences, especially noises and flashes of light have happened before but not of this magnitude.

The next morning, I went into the garden to check the grass under my studio window which is on the top floor of the house. There was absolutely nothing there. Nothing at all that might have produced the anomaly. There are no neighbours within the reach of the big walled garden all around my house. The nearest house is some 80 meters from the garden wall and there are woods in between.

While not exact, this cover reflects that event, one which will always be in my mind.

CONTENTS

INTRODUCTION

This is not a conventional book in the sense normally understood by the word. By that I mean it is not a story or a report. Rather it is a collection of thoughts, impressions, reflections and experiences of a person who has spent the past 20 years of her life pondering the issues of life and death and reflecting upon the information received by Instrumental Transcommunication (ITC) from her communicators who affirm to be "the dead speaking from another dimension beyond time".

I believe readers and people who have heard about the phenomenon will have numerous questions regarding the anomalous electronic voices. And rightly so, because the existence of the voices telling us they "speak from another world" means that a total upheaval of the standard science models, which we inherited and have lived with since we were born, is needed.

I will modestly attempt to throw some light onto a field that for the majority of people represents the unknown domain of obscure fantasy and disbelief. That is not to say that I can explain everything because neither I nor anybody else can do that. But I will attempt to widen the path of human understanding.

My purpose here is to produce a useful complement to my previous books on the subject. Although they are pretty comprehensive, the field is so vast and so intricate that much more remains to be said and that is what I will endeavour in this book.

I will deal with issues which, one way or another, have impressed me, particularly throughout the latter period of my life. I will focus on my impressions and the new way of thinking, which this amazing contact with voices, who claim to speak to us from "another dimension beyond time", has produced in me.

I will cite information apparently received telepathically from my communicators. This normally occurs in the form of a reply or unexpected comment without voice, thus, as a thought. I do not hear voices but if, for instance, I ask my communicators a question and keep very quiet, although not necessarily in a meditative state – just quiet and still, withdrawn from thought as much as possible – I can perceive information in response to my question, which has a different feel from my ordinary thoughts. It is soft and calm and it inspires me with a sense of tranquility and wellness. I must say that this method has improved with time and nowadays I can "speak" with my communicators at any time without any effort or special attitude. However, naturally enough, I cannot guarantee that the information I receive comes from my communicators, the Portuguese group at Rio do Tempo station,[1] and not from another universal source of knowledge. All I know is that I address them silently and I get replies, which most of the time prove to be correct. Furthermore, I must clarify that I never ask my communicators about the future. I would not feel comfortable if I did because I think it would not be ethically correct. But I must add that from time to time they have spontaneously given me clues about the development of a situation that has caused me great pain and distress, such as the serious illness of one of my beloved animal companions, and their information has invariably proved to be correct. In

---

[1]   My communicators state that they speak from Rio do Tempo (the Portuguese group) at a station (or transmitting centre) in the next level of life from where the most advanced contacts with the earth are broadcast.

some cases their information has been in total opposition to what the veterinarians, and I, expected. This has happened on many occasions.

Other ITC experimenters since Friedrich Jürgenson's time have reported similar experiences. For example at the Harsch-Fischbach's in Luxembourg, the Technician told Maggy Harsch that through ITC contacts she "had acquired mediumistic skills" (Locher and Harsch, 1989).

In the coming chapters I will speak of some strange experiences that I have had in the field of the supranormal, or paranormal as some would say although, in my opinion, that word is inexact. Everything is 'normal' but we ignore the largest and most significant majority of nature's events and, above all, her potentiality. I will endeavour to open further the path to the exploration, and comprehension, of the anomalous electronic voices.

Dr Konstantin Raudive, the remarkable deceased pioneer of Instrumental Transcommunication, purportedly conveyed from his new world to a French researcher, Aline Piget: "I would like you to know, dear Aline, that the object of an earthly life is not just the goodness. The object is to be conscious ... ." (Théry, P., 2000, *ITC Journal*, 2, pp 42-43).

From their side, my communicators from Rio do Tempo station told me years ago, "We speak to the world, everywhere, the opening of the way!"

Presently, my goal in life besides ITC experimentation and exploration is to contribute to the badly needed expansion of human consciousness. Presently, my communicators work tirelessly to better the communication, and, in their words, "to be able to speak to everybody in your world [ours] interested in our world [theirs]". When they are able to speak with me through the Direct Radio Voice (DRV) method they reiterate their goal loud and clear and every single time we speak telepathically. I sincerely hope this book will contribute to our common endeavour.

1

THE BACKGROUND

I was born and raised in Southern Europe and had a traditional, orthodox education and family upbringing. To give an example, I never heard anybody in my family speak about 'ghosts' or 'apparitions' except in a derisory tone. No one in my family nor acquaintances, in short, nobody I knew, took these issues seriously. Perhaps only my father wondered about them since from a very young age he had experienced what seemed to be out of body and other exceptional experiences. But considering the hostile reaction he would have faced in our traditional and restricted cultural environment, he dared not speak openly about these incidents, although he liked to read what he could find on the subject. Not much, I must say!

Thus, I am the heiress of a very conventional approach to any of the so-called paranormal phenomena, mainly inspired by my mother, a woman totally committed to rationality who truly disliked any suggestion of supranormal events. I am sure that my mother's worldview has conditioned me not to accept easily the phenomena, which have confronted me for decades. If I had to define myself I would say that I am a sceptic defeated by the evidence.

As mentioned in the Introduction, this book is not on Instrumental Transcommunication (ITC) per se, but rather on the impressions and thoughts, which I have experienced throughout the years since I became an ITC operator. However, I find it essential to offer my readers a brief summary of this contemporary method of attempting to contact another dimension of life, particularly for those who have not read my previous books or articles on the subject.

This fascinating area of psychical research has yielded results, which are strongly suggestive of the survival of consciousness after physical death, and seriously questions the prevailing materialistic paradigm of our time. The survival evidence provided by ITC takes the form of voices, images and texts recorded on electronic media by means still inexplicable to modern science.

My own research focuses chiefly on audio ITC. Consequently, I shall deal mainly with the voice phenomenon. There are two types of allegedly anomalous voices – firstly, EVP (short for Electronic Voice Phenomena), which sound to the ear like human voices that are recorded on magnetic tapes or digital devices, usually in reply to the operator's questions. They can be heard only when the recording is played back. Secondly, there are voices that emanate directly from the loudspeaker of a radio into the air, often in response to questions or comments from the human experimenter. These are known as DRV (Direct Radio Voices) and are much less frequent.

Both EVP and DRV appear to be produced by invisible communicators who, on the whole, identify themselves as deceased humans. The messages are received by both means but mainly DRV, which in some cases allow for significant dialogue and cover a large spectrum of information, some of which is previously unknown to the human experimenter. The identification of the communicator and other deceased individuals, detailed descriptions of the next world and high ethical teachings, have been reported.

The origin of audio ITC in its most popular form, the commonly known EVP, appears to go back to a Russian ethnographer,

Waldemar Bogoras who, in 1901, reported having heard the first example of voices of unexplained origin while recording the invocations of Chukchi shamans during an expedition to Siberia. The ethnographer himself reported on the occurrence in "The Chukchi Jesup North Pacific Expedition", Vol. 7, II, p. 435 (Grandsire, 1998).

Later, in the 1950s, anomalous electronic voices occurred spontaneously and almost simultaneously in Italy, Sweden and the USA. Father François Brune PhD, a French theologian and renowned psychical researcher, reported in his book, *Les Morts Nous Parlent* (1988) that on September 17, 1952, two eminent Catholic priests and scholars, Fathers Drs Agostino Gemelli (a prominent medical doctor and physicist) and Pellegrino Ernetti (a Benedictine from the famous Abbey of Saint Giorgio Maggiore in Venice), while working on Gregorian chants at the Experimental Laboratory of Physics of the Catholic University of Milan, recognised in one of the recordings the voice of Gemelli's father, who reportedly addressed his son personally. Flabbergasted, Gemelli decided to draw the matter to the attention of Pope Pius XII. Interestingly, the Pope had a very positive reaction and reassured them on the nature of the occurrence, declaring, for the peace of mind of the two highly bewildered and worried priests: "Do not worry Fathers! Your experience has nothing in common with Spiritism for tape recorders cannot be influenced. It can even mark the beginning of a new scientific study to confirm the faith in the Afterlife" (Brune, 1993).

But it is the Swedish artist and filmmaker Friedrich Jürgenson[2] who, quite rightly, is referred to as the father of anomalous electronic voice research. He recorded thousands of communications beginning in 1959, and made his discovery widely known in Europe, sparing no effort to publicise the phenomenon. Jürgenson committed his highly successful artistic career and personal life to this extraordinary discovery that totally changed his life (Jürgenson, 2004).

---

[2] Friedrich Jürgenson was the great pioneer of EVP and ITC.

Although as early as 1956, Attila von Szalay had already recorded EVP voices in the USA in collaboration with Raymond Bayless (Rogo and Bayless 1979), Jürgenson knew nothing about the phenomenon or even the existence of other experimenters. With intelligence, generosity and wisdom, Friedrich, affectionately called Friedel by the voices, brought the extraordinary phenomena to the attention of the world.

One of the academics who read about Jürgenson's experiences was Dr Konstantin Raudive, a prominent Latvian philosopher with published work to his credit. He started experimenting with Jürgenson and, although they went their separate ways a few years later, Raudive became a highly successful experimenter in his own right. Raudive was responsible for the rigorous scientific approach that ITC phenomena earned in his time (see his excellent book *Breakthrough* (1971), which includes technical and scientific reports of contemporary European scholars.

From its initial phase in the 1960s to the present day, a large amount of remarkable material, which includes clear photos of deceased personalities and complex computer texts of great significance, some of which are attributed to non-human high entities, have been received by researchers in continental Europe and elsewhere (Brune, 1993, 2005; Locher & Harsch, ibid 1989; Senkowski, 1995; Cardoso, 2010, 2017). Some of this information was reportedly unknown to anybody present during the experiments and its validity discovered by chance some time later. ITC contacts have rapidly become well established and continue to produce what seems to be impressive evidence of survival of physical death. Furthermore, they provide us with objective phenomena of great value and significance in its own right, quite apart from its relevance to the survival hypothesis.

In this book I will also quote from the communications received by Maggy and Jules Harsch-Fischbach in Luxembourg, Adolf Homes in Rivenich, Germany, Marcello Bacci in Grosseto, Italy as well as from other operators and sources. The former are among the most notable of the contemporary ITC researchers since Friedrich Jürgenson.

In my previous writings I have spoken extensively about Jules and Maggy Harsch-Fischbach of Luxembourg. Apparently, they are currently inactive in ITC work and cannot be reached; however, the communications they received, devised and directed by the high entity experimenters called the Technician with the collaboration of the deceased scientist of another physical world Swejen Salter, comprise what could be regarded as some of the most monumental information ever received from the next dimension of life. It came via DRV, computer texts, computer images and telephone calls. The circumstances and the amazing content of the messages, which completely contradict the current paradigm, regrettably compelled other ITC operators and the public in general to doubt their veracity, but many scientists who have witnessed and participated in the ITC sessions in Luxembourg don't doubt the authenticity of these awesome communications.

Adolf Homes from Germany followed in the footsteps of Maggy and Jules Harsch-Fischbach and the information he obtained is of a similar magnitude, although it came mostly via spontaneous computer texts, some of which were announced beforehand in Luxembourg in a kind of *the cross-correspondences* of the past. Homes is deceased but his wonderful work was closely followed by German physicist Professor Ernst Senkowski and most of the amazing communications that he received from other dimensions were compiled by him. Homes was a modest carpenter who often did not comprehend the meaning of the information he received, as he often told Prof. Senkowski.

Marcello Bacci, now deceased, didn't carry out any experiments in his last few years. His work, unique from the point of view of duration, yielded positive results for over 30 years. I was in Grosseto on a couple of occasions and witnessed the singular Direct Radio Voices at Bacci's studio. I even exchanged a few sentences with the communicators, some of them in Portuguese (see *ITC Journal* 25, 2006, pp.24-33).

Our friends in the next world have repeatedly insisted that the object of ITC is to achieve direct contact with the experimenters on the Earth, free from the interference of the mind of human mediums, with the purpose of conveying accurate information about their world and life conditions.

I think that methods used in the past by communicators who affirm to be from "the other world" have been tailored to the epochs concerned and the same is now true of ITC. Naturally, had it not been so, they would not have been understood by those whom they were intended for. Since the middle of the twentieth century, our civilization has quickly evolved into a technological society based principally on electronics. ITC, the term coined by Dr Ernst Senkowski, Professor of Physics, is the latest development in the communication between dimensions.

2

THE ELECTRONIC VOICES EXPERIENCE: SOME MISHAPS

The attitude of science

Modern science, predominantly materialist, has told us in many different ways that the existence of life after physical death is the mere speculation of misguided minds immersed in superstition – an invention of vivid imaginations with no credible basis. Currently, science is the highest recognised arbiter that few dare to oppose or even question. Nevertheless, I must concede that there is a basis for this attitude. Official science (the only accredited one) takes into consideration that which can be demonstrated empirically and measured. However, the anomalous electronic voices can be tested and are repeatable, although not always on demand. But in this regard orthodox scientists go further – they ignore the phenomenon, claiming that it can't be falsified and, thus, there is no "scientific evidence' in their eyes because scientific evidence demands a thorough study. With few exceptions, this is the general rule of scientific behaviour.

An invisible barrier has been erected against the existence of these strange electronic voices that so disturb the current paradigm. But the anomalous voices do exist and manifest themselves in many different locations throughout the world. In many cases the dialogue with the operators is clear. Their main message is basically the same: they tell us they "are the dead speaking from another world". And so we are in a dilemma! For the reasons mentioned above, the representatives of science have tacitly decided to ignore the phenomenon. Many parapsychologists in their desperate, albeit failed quest to obtain recognition from mainstream science, have done exactly the same.

In reality, the existence of the anomalous electronic voices has been denied without any testing or examination, a priori. It is a most unscientific approach that contradicts the foundations of science because the electronic voices, images and texts constitute objective evidence that can be analysed with the tools of modern science. In their own words: this was the main goal of the communicators when they devised this new method, which so far has been ineffectual for their purpose, notwithstanding the fact that on few occasions the tools of modern science were applied. This is what Professor Hans Bender did when he thoroughly investigated and studied the electronic voices obtained by Friedrich Jürgenson (Bender, 1970). From our side, during the EVP experiments carried out at the Laboratory of Acoustics of the School of Engineering, at Vigo University, the highest controlled conditions currently available were put into practice and all the same, positive results were obtained, (See Cardoso, 2012). Nevertheless, no scientist showed the slightest interest in reviewing the tests or examining the recordings.

Psychological barriers affect the operators

The difficulties brought about by the voices are many. Perhaps the main challenge, which can also affect the operators who receive them, is the full acceptance of their origin. Throughout the years I have recorded thousands of voices that replied to my requests for identification, affirming to be from my brother, father, mother, grandmother, grandfather, uncles and also from some of my beloved dogs, all of them deceased. They say, "We live in heaven, we are happy" and many other straightforward but, to us, incredible things. Many of the voices are clear, loud and unmistakable. The contents of their speech cannot be misinterpreted. I have had dialogues with the communicators and some have given their names, which in several cases were unknown to me. I have had communications that proclaimed, "We [they] are the Portuguese group at Rio do Tempo station". I have received and recorded magnificent chants by feminine and masculine singers who state that they are the dead from Rio do Tempo. I have witnessed and experienced many other seemingly impossible wonders.

Taking into account that nobody has yet offered an alternative plausible explanation to these mysterious voices, all that I said above, or even a small portion of it, should have been enough to convince me of the irrelevance of physical death. And indeed it has, but strangely, not to the point of making me disregard death, as I should, when faced with it; because I do grieve and despair, doubt and wonder about the whole situation, including the anomalous voices.

To be frank, although I have accepted that the voices and their message that the dead have not really died are true. I still question the reality of what happens, perhaps because it so dramatically contradicts what we were taught and what we experience in our normal everyday lives. By that, I mean that death is overpowering; it is devastating and extremely poignant. It is incomprehensible in some ways. I must confess that I do not manage to cope with death as well as I should, given my experience of speaking with the "dead", even though I realise I should. Moreover, I feel ashamed of my reaction because I certainly know that I am privileged to experience these communications, and experience them in the first person in a direct and intense way and without intermediaries.

While I certainly do not doubt the voices because they are undeniable, somehow their message has not been fully absorbed by my consciousness yet. To my great despair, I live in emotional conflict most of the time, principally because I feel that this attitude is not fair to my communicators. I sometimes envy my dearest friend, Father François Brune Ph.D., deceased some time now, and his indifference towards death, something he longed for. "The day of my death will be the most beautiful day of my life", he used to say. When he died, I felt so sad that I cried for a number of days and this in spite of the fact that I knew he longed for death. I used to travel to Paris to be with him and have had the immense pleasure of exchanging views with him on ITC and other phenomena that he had witnessed and studied all over the world. He was an indefatigable searcher of the unknown, although ITC was the dearest to his heart because of the impact that the voices produce on people who have lost a beloved one. The joy of the convincing evidence thus attained cannot be reached through any other manifestation of survival as many parents of deceased children have avowed.

My obstinate feelings of repulsion towards death, of which I cannot rid myself, put me in a most strange condition: from one side the voices yield evidence of the highest probative value; from the other side death haunts me with all its seemingly cruel consequences. I have difficulty in coping with death and thus grief sometimes is extreme. It is true that my frame of mind may depend on the day and the mood I am in and even on the people who are around me, but it is still disturbing. Many times the voices answer all my questions and resolve my doubts, but at other times I cannot overcome my uncertainty. On such occasions I feel awfully disappointed with myself, guilty and miserable because, indeed, I "have no right to be sad" as my communicators have told me. However, perhaps I suffer less than some other people but I do suffer.

It is when I feel depressed, very tired because the work is not easy, when life looks grey and somber in the interminable winter days of constant rain and fog of the place where I currently live, that I feel most disturbed. I may then question the whole process and ponder whether I was right when I decided to leave everything behind, including the prospect of a caring husband after my dramatic divorce, a busy social life, an affluent lifestyle, all the travelling that I so much enjoyed and so many other things that make life in this world comfortable and cheerful. I have deliberately committed my latter life – personal, professional and social – to the research and study of the anomalous voices with all the sacrifice and renunciation in material and social terms that the choice implied. Most of the time, I rejoice in it. On a few occasions I have doubts, although never real regrets.

The difficult task of an ITC operator

The solitude that this work entails is a tough issue that often becomes difficult to bear for several reasons. First of all, the number of people interested in the survival of physical death hypothesis is comparatively small these days. Much smaller still is the number of those who are seriously interested in the matter to the point of collecting serious information and studying the pertinent literature. This attitude is even more obvious in the case of technically backed contacts, i.e. ITC, which tend to discourage and perhaps intimidate ordinary people. The difficulty, which many have in accepting that such contacts are possible, constitutes a major setback. And, therefore, when, and if, we try to explain or even speak about such contacts, a barrier of social rejection often descends on us.

An ITC operator is truly at ease only among other ITC operators because they understand the difficulties and the problems that the situation entails. This limitation offers very restricted opportunities for sharing our magnificent experiences, something that represents one of the most cherished and gratifying occasions in our lives. My present home is in Galicia, a secluded region in the North-West of Spain, and here the electronic voices are ignored, ridiculed or defamed. Unfortunately, there is no opportunity for a rich exchange of experiences and events, and this adds to my solitude.

The role of the media

The media in general plays an important part in the negative social attitude that surrounds death. The quality of the information becomes poorer every day and the announcements of death are usually wrapped in a curtain of irremediable loss, rejection and termination. Few speak positively of death publicly; fewer even welcome death with the possible exception of those who commit suicide. The widespread denial of death is an odd attitude for something which is as natural as life but which, strangely, I share in spite of my direct comprehension of the possibility of survival of consciousness and the powerful evidence to that effect provided by the voices.

Perhaps, the fact that I have no Spiritualist or religious belief of any kind plays a role in this attitude. I believe that the powerful social rejection that surrounds the issue also contributes to the anguish that I (and perhaps other ITC operators) feel when faced with death in spite of our extraordinary life experiences. Somebody who is sure of survival of physical death can, nonetheless, experience enormous difficulties in keeping such confidence unshakable when plunged into an environment of constant denial and mockery. In my opinion, this constitutes one of the major setbacks encountered by the ITC operator. The great pioneer Friedrich Jürgenson, one of the figures I admire and love most in this field, experienced all the troubles that we do today, notwithstanding the fact that he was a figure of high artistic and social ranking, to whom Pope Paul VI assigned several tasks, some of them of a personal nature.

I hope that my confession helps readers to know that I do understand their doubts and queries, of which I am sure there will be many. In our materialistic world, particularly in the west, where we are bombarded daily with the misery of death and its horrendous, inexorable condition of termination and degradation, an occurrence to be avoided at any cost, it is particularly difficult to think in terms of "another world" and of "death does not exist" as our communicators happily affirm. But the evidence speaks for itself.

3

HOW IT ALL HAPPENED

We start experimenting with EVP

I t is time to introduce my own exploration of this fascinating field to the readers of this book. I have explained the story in more detail in one of my earlier works but I wish to offer a brief summary of the adventure to new readers as well.

At the beginning, we were a small group of three friends, two atheists and one agnostic, myself. Of the three people involved only Carlos Fernández had not endured grief. Both my friend Lola and I had been deeply struck by grief. Of the three, only Carlos had a technical background and only he knew about ITC.

It is true that I had read a couple of books on the subject but their content was of such an unlikely nature that I strongly considered the possibility that the whole thing was just a bad joke. I remember being so stunned by their stories that, at a certain point, I started thinking that the whole thing was a kind of parapsychological science-fiction tale. I also thought it was very cruel to bereaved people. Nowadays, I am sure that a number of people take the same view about my own books. However, the experiences I relate are a fact and I am sure the same applies to the majority of ITC reports by other experimenters.

A local parapsychologist, aware of Carlos' technical interest in ITC, because he was building a Kirlian camera for him, introduced Carlos to us. We contacted Carlos, who lives in Vigo, with the hope of finding somebody to help us with experiments in a field of which we were completely ignorant. Carlos brought his technical background and some practical knowledge of ITC based on the Spanish exploration of this field, to our small group.

At the time, EVP was quite famous in Spain where it had acquired dramatic, terror-like tints, which I dislike very much because they bear no relationship to the facts.

The communications are not based on fear or horror but love.

We started experimenting at my house near Vigo.

Because Carlos lived nearby, it was easy to organise the meetings and EVP experiments. Lola came from near La Coruña where she was a teacher, at the time. Details of these first tests are in my book *Electronic Voices, Contact with Another Dimension?* and, therefore, I will not go over them here.

Our first results

When we started to obtain replies in response to our questions, I could not hide my surprise. I had never before had any contact with the so-called paranormal and it seemed even more fantastic to me. It is true that I have been fascinated by the possibilities of exploring the unknown from a young age. I remember, for example, that in my early teenage years, Louis Pauwels' and Jacques Bergier's *Le Matin des Magiciens* (*The Morning of the Magicians*, 1968, Stein and Day, Inc., Avon Books) was a source of great excitement for me, but I had not had any personal experience with anomalous phenomena before.

Our first results took place relatively quickly in the form of EVP voices, many of them loud and clear.

We carried on regularly and soon I became the most enthusiastic member of the group. The joy but also the bewilderment, which these extraordinary voices brought me, was indescribable. The world I knew crumbled into pieces and a new, entirely unknown reality opened up to me. Nothing could have been more important or caused a greater impact on my life.

I absolutely adored those mysterious voices and, in spite of the fact that I had had no previous contact whatsoever with the phenomenon, they did not really frighten me. I suppose the attraction for something as mystifying as a loud, clear voice of unknown origin that replies to you and cannot be heard when it does (only later in the recording playback), by far overcame the very legitimate concern that the situation could have caused to a person like me. I was not only unacquainted with the phenomenon but also not convinced of its reality.

At the beginning, a couple of guttural utterances almost frightened me. A good example is the loud EVP "O pai vive" (The father lives) in response to my appeal to Carlos de Almeida, who would become my main communicator, to tell my beloved father that I missed him very much.

This is a most extraordinary EVP not only because of the deep quality of the masculine voice that replied to my tearful request, but also because of the noises that accompanied it. The sound of heavy footsteps and a bang similar to the closing of a door, not produced in my recording studio or anywhere in the house or outside, could be heard loudly and unmistakably after the voice. The recording was done when only I was at my house, located in a secluded spot in the countryside. The odd sound of a door closing in this recording brings to my mind the communicators' frequent remarks about the "passage", a recurrent topic in their speech. I should explain that the tone of the voice, although it frightened me, was not menacing or distressing; it was just strange. However, it was a loud, guttural, and above all unexpected masculine voice and I am sure this is what scared me then, just a few months after we started our experiments.

The EVP "O pai vive" was recorded at the end of April 1998 and when I now listen to it, I find nothing scary about it. On the other hand, the last word, "vive", even sounds tenderly to me these days. Undoubtedly surprise must have been the main culprit of the shock I suffered at the time!

And then ... the Direct Radio Voices!

By far the most incredible experience of my life came about with the breathtaking DRV (Direct Radio Voices). The first of these happened on March 11, 1998, a couple of months after the first EVP, and since then my joy but also the perplexity caused by such extraordinary events attained levels of which I had never dreamt.

This was a miracle! Something I never really believed could happen and certainly not to me! I understand my rational education and conventional family upbringing were responsible for some scepticism towards the phenomenon, which kept troubling me. It was unavoidable; something I could not stop thinking about. Like all prejudices, this attitude was part of my nature and, occasionally, I still have to fight it.

Carlos and Lola had similar reactions to mine. The three of us had no connections to Spiritualist, Spiritist or any paranormal related traditions or beliefs and we shared similar Western education and conventional family backgrounds. We were soon trapped in the spell of the mysterious voices that replied to our questions powerfully and consistently, seemingly coming from nowhere.

After a short time, the voices seemed to favour the radio's loudspeaker as a way to communicate with me, which produced a mixture of incredulity and awe in my mind. 'This cannot be happening', was the recurrent thought with which I went to bed and awoke. I even used to wake up in the middle of the night and think that something must be wrong; something that did not fit. Maybe I was dreaming? But then the precise intonation of Carlos de Almeida's voice almost shouting and telling me, among other things, that he was "listening to everything", that it was "very, very difficult" [to speak through the radio], and that he was speaking from "another world" clearly resonated in my head. On those occasions, which were frequent, my heart would beat frantically, my body would shake vigorously and, in a way, I sometimes wished that I had not experienced such a fantastic event. I will remind my readers that genuine and comprehensible DRV is considered the rarest event, not only in the field of ITC but also in the entire field of parapsychology. Nowadays the knowledge that it exists is more widespread but when I started experimenting there were only a few cases in the world, namely, Marcello Bacci, Maggy and Jules Harsch-Fischbach and Adolf Homes. That is one reason why people from all over the world came to my house to learn about the phenomena.

The events, which we were privileged to encounter, by far exceeded most people's imagination including Carlos Fernández' who had already written a book on Psychotronics (Fernández, 1995) and wrote several others since our tests with the electronic voices.

Our weekly recording sessions, followed by an informal dinner at my house, were memorable gatherings where we listened to earlier recordings, planned the recording of the night and discussed the content of messages we had received.

Some of the voices sounded so natural, a quality that still strikes me today, and created a feeling of great wonderment for all of us. The word "magnificent" comes to mind when I think about this initial period and I wish that everybody could experience a similar situation because it is truly a life-changing event.

Naturally, after receiving thousands of communications, things have changed and, although I feel still enthralled by the DRV, I can now go to sleep peacefully after a session, something unthinkable in 1998. I continue to experience the magic of the voices every single time they get through, but I no longer feel the 'impossibility' of it all.

Recently, a perceptive acquaintance wrote to me as follows, " ... It must be very exciting when you switch your radios on and receive a response. I suspect that even after all these years it still has a profound effect on you." He was absolutely right!

One of the things that puzzled me at the beginning was the reason why we, the small group of three friends, were the recipients of the communications. The need for a motive for everything was ever-present in my way of thinking. This used to be a marked feature of my reasoning but now I understand (at least theoretically), that – perhaps in other levels of consciousness – there may not be reasons we understand for everything, at least the reasons we associate with cause and effect. From their side, my Rio do Tempo communicators once replied to a question I put to them on behalf of Professor David Fontana: "Why do some operators get results and others do not?" with "It depends on Rio do Tempo [therefore on them]".

But Friedrich Jürgenson was more specific and gave his personal view on the subject in reply to a question that a journalist put to him during an interview:

Question 7: Mr. Jürgenson, can you give a rational explanation why precisely you have been selected for this path-breaking work and what were the reasons that motivated you to suddenly give up your artistic career?

Answer: First of all, I would like to counter this question with one of my own, a question that I have already asked hundreds of my visitors, and that I now direct to readers of this book.

Would you be willing to give up your profession and leave your comfortable home in the city to bury yourself in isolation in the countryside to devote all your resources, strength and time to a really dubious kind of research that consists of getting to the bottom of some mystical and initially barely audible voices that appeared seemingly by accident on an audio tape?

As you already know, this is exactly what I did out of a clear, inner conviction. The fact that I was willing to reorganise my life completely both externally and internally was of great, but not decisive significance. Much more was required: an entire series of inbred and acquired capabilities that motivated the dead to entrust this difficult task to no one but me.

My endowment by nature, with a very sensitive ear and good musical talent along with the fact that I spoke five languages relatively fluently and had a working knowledge of three others was an essential precondition. Otherwise I could not have understood the multilingual shouts and communications of the dead. I also have the gift of concentration and psychic relaxation (meditation).

I have been occupied my entire life with the problem of death. In my youth I studied religion and philosophy thoroughly for five years. I did not fail to become closely acquainted with theosophy, the cabbala, yoga and anthroposophist teachings. I did this in a country in which all religious movements were persecuted ruthlessly, and I risked losing my freedom because of my secret studies as I had formed a small esoteric group. At the same time I could not avoid becoming acquainted with the basic theses of the Marxist dialectic.

I owe it on the one hand to my insatiable desire for knowledge, but on the other hand also to those chaotic external conditions that thickened the atmosphere, which made it possible for me to analyse the different ideologies thoroughly, and to free my mind from the all of the single-track doctrines and dogmas.

As a result of these studies, as a witness and victim of two world wars and of a destructive revolution, I discovered the source of the failures and sufferings of humanity. I started to look at life candidly and without prejudice and I was pained deeply by the suffering of humanity. Most of all, I recognised that all our anxieties and miseries could not be eliminated until we had incontestably solved the problem of death. All this, too, might have contributed to the reasons why it was me who was chosen to build the bridge between our world and the beyond." (Jürgenson, 2004, p. 102-103).

Without false modesty, I confess that I share many of the attributes highlighted by the 'Father of the Voices', namely the natural good ear and the polyglot abilities (both are associated) but above all the desire to discover the truth beyond human beliefs and conventional mental models.

In an encounter with the great American researcher of the Spiricom, George Meek, described in John Fuller's interesting book, *The Ghost of 29 Megacycles*, Jürgenson spoke about his work with the electronic voices. "You have to have great dedication for this work", he said. "And there are four basic requirements. First, you must have time – plenty of it. Second, you must have patience – an incredible amount of it. Third, you must have money, money to assemble equipment, discard what doesn't work, and buy more to replace it. But", Jürgenson added, "the most important thing of all is the willingness to take ridicule and slander". Fuller goes on to say that "Meek was in total agreement with Jürgenson's opinion and he found that Jürgenson's dedication to the EVP puzzle was intense. Like Meek, he felt that an electronic voice bridge would solve the puzzle of death for the first time in history… . " (Fuller, 1985).

Is there a cause-effect rule for ITC voices to happen?

I can ponder the possibility that cause and effect may not be tied together, although we are certainly under the impression that an effect is the result of a certain cause. But is it really or, at any rate, is it the direct result of the single cause that we have in mind? Could it be that the effect exists in parallel with the many potential causes and is just one of numerous possibilities, which occur at a given moment?

The wind blows and an apple falls from a tree. Naturally, our tendency will be to say that the wind caused the apple to fall. But can we be sure that the apple fell because of the wind? Maybe it fell down at that precise moment because it was ripe and would have fallen down anyway. Was there a tiny earth tremor, which imperceptibly shook the ground causing the apple to fall? I could carry on with this reasoning but the point is – was there a singular reason why the apple fell from the tree? If we think there is, we still have to find out precisely why the apple fell at that specific moment. And this is not an easy task because there were numerous potential reasons; therefore we cannot categorically attribute one specific cause to the effect we witnessed.

What if there wasn't a specific cause? Could it be that it was predetermined that the apple would fall down at that moment as postulated by fatalism? I know this hypothesis is rejected by science but even in science there are many exceptions to the golden rule of cause and effect.

With this in mind, we should also ponder what the deceased Konstantin Raudive affirmed in Luxembourg at Maggy and Jules Harsch-Fischbach's home. Present on the occasion were Luxembourg journalists, François Brune and Dr Senkowski. "December 4, 1988 (clear speech by DRV).

Dear friends, here speaks Konstantin Raudive. On the wrong track gets only he who tries to make a causal connection, (for) this does not exist. The basic error of the as yet prevailing material science with you, is that you try to apply the law of cause and effect, which is correct within a limited area of your existence, to all appearances, also to such where it has no validity. Look into today's condition of the world: extreme appearances in men's lives, extreme appearances in nature ... (connection breaks off)". (Senkowski, 1995).

When I lived in Lisbon, I had a maid, Maria Zulmira, who would give what I thought was a good reply to anybody who said things like: "such or such person died because of pneumonia, or because of cancer, or he had an accident" etc. She would invariably reply, "Death always has an excuse!" This logic is a good example of what I wish to convey about the possible motives for the voices to talk to me or anyone else.

Maybe there were no reasons or maybe there were many reasons; in reality we do not know for sure. I am perfectly aware that many operators enjoy giving the impression that they are the recipients of anomalous electronic communications because, as they put it, they are "psychic" or "mediumistic" or "the Spirits guided me to do it" and so on. Personally, I do not subscribe to such claims, which I particularly dislike. I reiterate that I have never followed the Spiritualist or the Spiritist movements. Not because I have any particular antagonism towards any of them but for the reason that, as Friedrich Jürgenson so well put it, "I do not belong to any political party, religious sect, secret fraternity or any other "ism" – like movements or directions" (Jürgenson, 2004).

Nevertheless, the communications that I receive validate some of the principles of said movements and I find it fair to acknowledge the fact. Indeed, to my knowledge, all anomalous electronic communications – EVP, DRV or even anomalous computer texts and images, as well as anomalous telephone calls – provide evidence for the survival of consciousness after physical death, and form the main principle of Spiritualism and Spiritism.

This confirmation started with Friedrich Jürgenson's messages. The Swedish man of art and culture did not know that these communications could happen and therefore, he was thunderstruck by the voices telling him they were "the dead".

My understanding that things are not necessarily what they seem and that the rule of cause-effect is not sacrosanct, came about as a result of the electronic voices. I have learned that we cannot understand it all and, even less, explain it all. Regrettably, every now and then, people who believe all so-called paranormal phenomena, even if not properly demonstrated to be true, accuse me of being sceptical. I am not sceptical as anybody who knows me or my work must concur, but I truly prefer to be an open-minded sceptic than a gullible spectator of fake scenarios with paranormal tints.

The idea that all anomalous phenomena are real is, in my opinion, as damaging to real anomalous phenomena as avowing that they are all deceitful and, therefore, garbage or, as hardline sceptics say, "such things do not exist". For me, nothing is more important than questioning – in normal life most certainly – even more so, in the field of anomalous experiences. Questioning is the foundation of sound judgment. This was certainly what Carlos and I did to the point of exhaustion with Rio do Tempo's DRV voices.

Although I consider that our human perspective, which varies constantly with time and so many other factors, must be only a minute portion of perhaps infinite-sided reality, it is still difficult for me to fully accept the reality of these strange, mind boggling voices and the messages they impart.

Seemingly, they originate in the next level of existence – another dimension, as our communicators sometimes call it. But our mental patterns are powerful and deep-rooted. They have mixed origin – inherited, cultural, geographic, and social. Thus, when I think of the extremely odd events that happened in my life, I must overcome that heritage and this is not easy. Also, when I was a little girl, I was invariably scolded and mocked if I showed the slightest interest toward the so-called paranormal phenomena. When the electronic voices unexpectedly started, this heavy psychological background must have weighed on me and my worried questions about what was happening never stopped. As my main communicator, Carlos de Almeida, remarked many years ago via the DRV, "I called you through the old radio [but] you are in such confusion!" Indeed, my confusion was enormous.

I am sure that the expansion of consciousness, considered by our dear communicators to be humanity's utmost need, plays a decisive role in our capacity to accept the apparently impossible. Recently, I saw a renowned astrophysicist, whose name I cannot recall, paraphrase Heraclitus in a TV interview to explain his point: "He who does not expect will not find the unexpected". As with my house cleaner's logic, I think it is useful to keep this suggestion in mind when we think about the phenomenon and all the unknown aspects involved in its manifestation.

Questioning the origin of the voices

Thus, the odd situation I went through and what it apparently meant – the survival of consciousness after physical death – seemed so very improbable to me that it drove me not to accept the anomalous origin of the EVP and, even more clearly, of the DRV we, and later I, alone, received. For over a year I searched incessantly, albeit in vain, for a normal explanation.

For this task, I worked with the technical help of Carlos Fernández, an electronics technician by education interested in anomalous phenomena, as I have already indicated. Carlos could be classified as a sceptic, but, more accurately, I would define him as an open-minded sceptic. In his book, he admits to this, very particularly with regard to the Direct Radio Voices (Fernández, 2006).

We examined the possibility of receiving communication from fishing boats, ham radio operators and police radios; Carlos, with the help of friends and acquaintances more directly involved in those areas, examined all. None was found responsible for the DRV.

Police, aviation personnel and fishermen who use radio would not respond to the questions, which I ask inside my studio in a rather secluded house on the top of a hill, for the simple reason that they cannot hear what I ask or say. I do not have a radio transmitter. Moreover, the semantics of the voices cannot be mistaken for fishing, aviation or police radio communications, nor for normal radio transmissions.

R. V., a senior researcher in physics, then a lecturer of physics at the University of Santiago de Compostela, and a researcher of EVP/DRV, thoroughly examined the frequencies used by Rio do Tempo for the DRV; R. V. (he prefers to remain anonymous because of his professional status) concluded that all of them are radio frequencies reserved for State use (see *ITC Journal* nº 41 and 42).

The Super ESP hypothesis

It was only when one of a number of parapsychologists offered his own interpretation based upon Super-ESP (e.g. Barušs, I., 2011) that again I questioned the phenomenon. This does not mean that their arguments convinced me but they made me ponder them and perhaps that was a positive approach because their hypothesis should be taken into consideration.

Friedrich Jürgenson also commented on some parapsychologists' favourite classification of the voices – auditory delusions – and their suggestion that "The voices are the result of the unconscious psychokinetic action of the operator". Jürgenson wisely remarked that if his mind had such powers, he "would certainly be the most powerful man on Earth" (Jürgenson, 2004). Indeed, how could it be that the "unconscious psychokinetic action of the operator" could produce thousands of different voices modulated on radio waves – some masculine, some feminine, some childlike, some clearly electronic-sounding but others emotional or very serene, some very beautiful who speak with the operator jokingly or seriously or metaphorically? In addition, how could it produce chants and music of a singular nature and so many other strange things?

At some point I did ponder the psychokinetic hypothesis myself, but in no way can I accept it because it would be an even more bizarre and improbable explanation than acknowledging that the communicators are who they say they are. Thus, I concur with Jürgenson's remarks until a more convincing hypothesis comes along.

4

REFLECTIONS ON DEATH

~

I shared some thoughts about the daunting part of life we call death at the beginning of this book and, although running the risk of repeating myself, I will recount minutely the most pressing feelings I experience in this regard.

Nothing in life has ever puzzled me more than death. I could never manage to comprehend it, although I have learned a great deal about the subject during the last 20 years through my own and other ITC operators' work.

For most of us, death is an extremely dramatic, dreadful event as is the dying process that precedes it. Indeed, great faith is necessary to witness death, particularly when it involves suffering, and continue to believe in the reality of survival. Although I am privileged to receive objective evidence of it through ITC, it does not manage to fully quieten my spirit when death strikes on my door.

I have a friend in Italy who lost her only young son, as well as her husband, father, sister, brother and brother-in-law, and yet is capable of assuring others of her total confidence in the survival of physical death with these words:

I think that death is absolutely the most beautiful moment of life and how can we cry when the people we love have the possibility of experiencing this joy? ... My son, Stefano, when he had a physical body was my paladin; he was the friend that understood and sustained me; he was my second youth. However, when he left I was happy for him ... (Aimone Querio, 2012, *Dalla loro parte*, p. 22).

Lorenza, my Italian friend, is a committed Christian of admirable faith. She is also a successful EVP operator, but she did not need the assurance provided by her electronic messages to build her faith. She already had it. I have another friend in Lisbon who is not an EVP operator and suffered great losses through death. He says he does not need any extra proof because he is "a man of faith". I admire and, to a certain extent, I envy people like them.

The admirable Friedrich Jürgenson had these wise words about death in his book *Voice Transmissions with the Deceased* (2004):

Ignorant humanity stands before an invisible abyss, before a cruel emptiness "from which no one has as yet returned", as the popular saying goes, a heart filled with terror, grief and fear. And now a dead person speaks on tape to his friend! Someone who disappeared into the "Great Nothingness" speaks clearly with his old, dear voice clearly and always repeatable on a tape – in spite of infarct, cremation and that small pile of ashes, the presence of which is also undeniable.

This realisation filled my entire being with boundless, exuberant joy.

It seemed to me that I had turned suddenly, once again, into a little boy whose carefree lightheartedness knew no bounds.

I don't remember any more how long this joyful intoxication lasted based on the unshakable certainty that this simple, brownish tape carried the voice of immortality undeniable by any worldly authority (p. 77).

Jürgenson does not say how long the awe lasted, if it was until a further shock caused by the death of another beloved friend or if it never left him, as I suppose was the case; but he was an exceptional human being, an enlightened man of a different kind from many of us.

The great transcommunicator Adolf Homes received numerous messages about death, chiefly in the form of computer texts conveyed by higher entities that purportedly belonged to higher spheres of existence. Although Maggy and Jules Harsch-Fischbach also received messages in the form of computer texts transmitted mainly by the high entity whom they called the Technician, and Swejen Salter, Homes' computer messages were of such magnitude that we might rightly classify them as an event unparalleled in the history of ITC. I translate an extract from the Italian translation of Prof. Senkowski's compilation of Homes' messages (in German).

Do not fear death because it does not exist. God will liberate man and animal from the terrors of death. Animal and man, death cannot keep hold of you. With the physical end of the individual the programmed consciousness changes. Your present consciousness is malleable, therefore after your physical death you will change until at some point, you experience the [for you], infinite cosmos. After your physical death, you will be completely free and past and future will be visible [to you]. In the regions of our existence a pleasant world awaits you. When you join us, you will have many possibilities of advancing also in other planes and worlds..." (Senkowski original version, pp. 85-86; Italian translation, p. 80).

The above text is only a paragraph from a long chapter on Homes' computer messages about death. Several concepts caught my attention in this message, the main one being that our "programmed consciousness" will be transformed after death and "After your physical death, you will be completely free". These statements could drive us to question chance and, above all, free will. Personally, I do not think free will is as free as we think. Perhaps it exists in trivial situations but in my opinion not in all. These are thoughts, which, of course, I cannot substantiate but neither can the advocates of free will substantiate theirs. Seemingly we, humans, possess and exercise free will, but do we really? Again, I think that conviction is a manifestation of a paradigm eminently anthropocentric.

The truth is that our world appears more like a virtual cosmic experience than a real world to me. If my musing were correct, all would make sense including the "programmed consciousness" announced by the high entities and even physical death.

Jürgenson also speaks of the major transformation after death:

> This is not to say that all the dead persons are suddenly transformed into pure angels. The decisive transformation that took place in the psyche of the deceased only depends to a certain extent on the deliverance from their frail human bodies. The most significant role is played by the influence of their dimension outside time and space, a synchronicity that affords the dead the great advantage of direct perception. The practical results of this timeless perception can only be perceived with difficulty from our perspective, or not at all for most of us" (Jürgenson, 2004, p. 145).

Many years ago, long before I read Jürgenson's book, I asked Rio do Tempo if the marvelous capabilities, which they enjoy in their new world and about which I spoke at length in other works, were obtained through the death process. They replied: "They pertain to our world [theirs]". Another similarity of great significance.

Similarities, or convergent information, represent a point of great interest in the study of the evidence offered by our discipline. The matching explanations contained in the messages received in different places of the world by different operators who had no contact with each other, validate the mindboggling content of the communications and a reassuring common pattern emerges. The next world acquires a hint of reality no matter how different it may be from our present world. We realise that we are not dreaming a science-fiction movie!

The fear of death

In an interview with the American spiritual teacher Ram Dass, David Marchese asked:

> You've said that you're ready to die. When did you know?

> When I arrived at my soul. Soul doesn't have fear of dying. Ego has very pronounced fear of dying. The ego, this incarnation, is life and dying. The soul is infinite. (*New York Times* magazine, September 2, 2019).

The whole interview is a great example of wisdom but I found his explanation of death and the soul the most enlightening way of describing two major concerns of the human mind.

Although I personally do not fear death, at least not consciously, I believe fear certainly plays a role in the widespread human attitude of repulsion and denial of death but it is not its only cause.

Years ago, shortly before my beloved Doberman dog Barbara Lady left me, somebody from Rio do Tempo station told me in the typical language of the voices (literal translation): "When she dies from our side, you do not have the right to be sad!" This admonition rightly reflects what I feel when I grieve, something that happens more often than I would like but which I cannot avoid because I am an animal lover and in general the non-human animals that live with us have shorter lives than humans. I do grieve for them as much, often more, than I do for my human friends. I am very sensitive to their innocence and to their tender vulnerability.

When the sad time comes to watch their physical suffering (which sometimes seems more intense than in humans) and their passing, I feel great distress. And when the time of those who live with me comes, the pain is so intense that words cannot describe it. A wave of despair and repulsion against life engulfs me and I do not know what to do. I feel lost because I think that little innocent animals, guilty of no harm, so full of love and joie de vivre, should not have to endure the tremendous suffering and agony, which some of them are destined to bear. To me, that appears not only horrendous but also extremely unfair. I would like them simply to transit sweetly and easily into the next level of life as our communicators call it. I wish that with all my heart but, sadly, it rarely happens. I recall the words of Rio do Tempo about the role of suffering: "it is very important; it is highly significant" and then I think that maybe it is as they say but the pain remains and I cannot ignore it.

Another type of communication, this time through the mediumship of the great clairvoyant Marcel Belline, purportedly in contact with his deceased son Michel, conveyed a similar reflection about suffering: "Suffering, adversities are necessary to [reach] understanding, they inevitably hit the best who are the most vulnerable" (Belline, 1972, p. 133).

I have offered my readers the example of my dearest Lady – 20 years later, the memory of her departure still makes me cry. Why does this happen? I know that she is well because my communicators have told me so on innumerable occasions and I do trust them. Furthermore, some years ago, on one of the occasions I spoke about her during my ITC session, a faint, little girlish voice uttered "Lady!", and I believe it was from her. It made me extremely happy but I still cannot stop being sad. I suppose this is because I miss her physical presence, and because in the recesses of our mind (I speak in the plural because I believe it applies to most of us), in spite of the powerful evidence of great quality offered by the ITC voices, which can be heard by anybody, we still waver – such is the strength of our doubt. Can we free ourselves from these devastating feelings? I doubt it because as long as we live in the physical body we cannot release ourselves entirely from our physical connections, even if we know, as I do, that all beings survive death. I mean the physical connection is visceral and extremely powerful. Moreover, we absorb the information, which our beloved, deceased ones convey to us via our brain, not through our gut. In our dimension the gut is more powerful than the brain because it is inborn, while our brains develop throughout life. Death we see, we touch, we smell, but survival of consciousness we do not!

We rejoice but still doubt!

The delight I experience when I listen to my communicators comes with an overpowering sense of wonderment. A feeling of immense gratitude overcomes me, makes me tremble and cry and everything falls into place. Suddenly all is well as if a miracle had happened. I recall an EVP voice recorded by Monique et Jacques Blanc-Garin of the French Association Infinitude, which uttered "Nous sommes là, mais c'est pas un miracle!" (We are there but it is not a miracle!). They certainly know best!

Friedrich Jürgenson said:

> With the increase of new transmissions, my interest and enthusiasm grew literally day-by-day. The connection that had developed between my friends and me was of such unusual kind despite its clear and undeniable evidential character that in reality I never really got used to it and I always found myself anew in a state of wonderment. (Jürgenson, ibid, 2004 p. 119).

I could not agree more. Unfortunately the whole process of doubt versus joy restarts a few days later.

I believe that one of the factors, which plays a major role in our concern about our dear deceased ones, even though we listen to loud messages, seemingly from them, is not being absolutely sure that indeed they go on living and are well. Nevertheless, how could we be absolutely sure? The voices tell us "The dead are alive, always", "We are very happy!" – "It is your father João Cardoso" and similar statements, but we cannot see them, touch them, smell them, hug them and so on. We hear them, it is true, and believe what we hear but sometimes we ask ourselves, are they really who and what they say they are? Regrettably and very unfairly, sometimes I still doubt. Our mind will always contradict our heart ... such is human nature.

Let me clarify what I mean when I say that we, ITC operators, 'are privileged' to receive voices from another dimension. This experience is definitely a major privilege because what else could be more important than to speak directly and objectively with those who live in another dimension and who, in addition, are also our deceased loved ones (if that happens to be the case)? It does not occur because we have more merit than others but perhaps because we are able to do it, "... with all our heart, all our mind and all our body, this is the melting pot that is useful ... it is necessary to try ... it is different fields ... ". This was how a DRV voice replied to a question put to Bacci's communicators by Silvana Pagnotta's husband at the centre in Grosseto. He had asked about the possibility of obtaining a direct personal contact with them (Capitani and Pagnotta 1990, p. 55).

The soothing power of the voices

When I manage to put my rational frame of mind aside and make the leap beyond common sense, what the communicators say is instantly absorbed by me without logical considerations of any kind. It is an instinctive reaction, a kind of recognition of the truth in a visceral way. I would call it the truth of the heart.

On those occasions, the overwhelming joy produced by the voices makes me want to yell and jump like a child. Other kinds of survival evidence that I have experienced have not had the same effect. Is this one of the reasons why I am an ITC operator? I think that perhaps it is.

However, when later on in the quiet of my office, free from the spell of the voices I ponder their contents – a masculine voice saying it is my brother, Luís, deceased in 1996, or a gentle, feminine, childlike voice that utters: "I am Nisha!", my beloved Doberman dog, Lady's mother, my mind shouts: Oh my goodness, this is crazy, this cannot be true!

An English friend, an intelligent and cultured man who is not fluent in Portuguese but has some notion of the pronunciation, remarked in a letter he wrote to me about my CD 'Electronic Voices':

> ... We have started listening to the CD. How can anyone ever suggest they are stray radio transmissions!! While the voices may not be "human" but "electronic" reconstructions, they have a human/soul quality that is self-evident. Often, they display a sense of determination to get their message over by the obvious effort they are making. No wonder you reacted as you did!

I was surprised by the way he caught the spirit of the voices and how he went straight to the point in his remarks because, indeed, the voices' endeavor is unmistakable and very moving. Recently, a masculine voice painfully articulated in one of Rio do Tempo's long working sessions which I described elsewhere: (translation) "... [this is] your father, the voice of effort!". When I hear it, tears pour down my face. How could it be any different? The voice is clear, what it says is beyond any doubt for any native of my language, and this is my deceased father speaking to me with enormous effort!

We cannot feel the transcendence of life

Once a commanding direct radio voice, which I ascribed to the Technician, uttered, "Dare, always dare!" This happened when I was speaking to voices that had pleaded for help the day before. I never found out if it was speaking to me or to the voices begging for help. Maybe it was for both. However, this is certainly what we need to do in our world: dare and "set fire to minds" as an outstanding deceased scientific personality advised the Luxembourg operators and the participants in the DRV session.

The scientist, the nineteenth century French chemist Henri Sainte-Claire Deville, uttered an entirely clear message:

> My name is Henry Sainte Claire Deville. I left your world in 1881, and I am speaking to you in my name and in the name of our staff from LIFELINE, the scientists. Your project as well as [those] from LIFELINE and from TIMESTREAM is to set fire to minds, to set fire to minds in your world, and in that moment to try to master time. I can give you a few explanations.
>
> The void dreams the universe, but the void is unconscious …

The long message continues and I had the privilege of listening to it directly from Professor Ernst Senkowski's recording. Together with other scientists, he was present in Luxembourg on this memorable occasion (See Cardoso, 2017, pp. 65-67).

The intelligibility of this voice, as many other DRVs received in Luxembourg, is total. There is no place for ambiguity in the interpretation.

We would, perhaps, be able to look at death from the point of view recommended by Adolf Homes' ITC partners, admittedly high entities from another dimension: "We beg you [us on the earth] to learn to reflect that you have to die there [here in our world] to advance, because you live in the span of an illusion, which we call time" (Senkowski, 1999, Italian translation, p. 79).

As William Blake admirably remarked, "if the doors of perception were cleansed, everything would appear to man as it is, infinite". Then, perhaps we would be able to feel the infinity of life. We would be able to understand the full meaning of George Sand's message to a close friend grieving for her only son's death. At the end of her consolation letter to Marie Dorval, Sand wrote:

> There is no madness or stupidity in believing in a better life to where the ones who preceded us travel and where we will reunite with them. For me it would be impossible not to believe in it, and those I have lost and loved appear always living to me. If death were something absolute life would not exist... (Belline, 1978, p. 243).

After we die we will experience the infinite, as the high entities told Adolf Homes. In our current condition we cannot perceive the infinite but our communicators, at least some of them, can. As my beloved Filipe from Rio do Tempo station told me years ago, among other moving statements "... and I feel another colour, I feel my power of infinity..." (See CD Electronic Voices, www.itcjournal.org; Cardoso, 2017).

Will this power of infinity be the outcome of the divine connection in a more advanced stage of existence, namely the next world? Very likely so. But who, or what, is God? Certainly the Principle of all that is as the Technician told the experimenters in Luxembourg; and Hildegard Schäfer,[3] herself a successful ITC operator, when she asked for a comment about God, received from her voices this straightforward reply: "God is in us". (Schäfer, 1992, French ed. p. 322).

Great human minds, in this case Giordano Bruno, one of the greatest, had similar thoughts centuries ago:

---

[3] Hildegard Schäfer was a remarkable ITC researcher, experimenter and author in the last century. She published several excellent books that anybody interested in our discipline should read. They are extremely informative, serious and clear.

Nature is none other than God in things ... Animals and plants are living effects of Nature; whence all of God is in all things ... Think thus, of the sun in the crocus, in the narcissus, in the heliotrope, in the rooster, in the lion" "The universe comprises all being in a totality; for nothing that exists is outside or beyond infinite being, as the latter has no outside or beyond." And, "Divinity reveals herself in all things... everything has Divinity latent within itself. For she enfolds and imparts herself even unto the smallest beings, and from the smallest beings, according to their capacity. Without her presence nothing would have being, because she is the essence of the existence of the first unto the last being. (Bruno, 1584)

I could go on recalling the thoughts of one the greatest figures who ever lived on this earth and one whom I admire and love the most.

5

MY ENCOUNTER WITH DEATH AND OTHER MOVING EXPERIENCES

My childhood and the awful discovery of death

When I was around six years old, my first direct experience of death came through the passing of a female turkey that I very much liked. I have been very fond of animals for as long as I can remember.

The years of my childhood and youth were joyful and extremely happy. I spent most of the time with my maternal grandparents whom I adored, in their big, lovely estate full of animals, flowers, trees, vegetables and even a wonderful patch of forest. My grandparents were wealthy people and I remember those years, the happiest of my whole life, as if I had been floating on a sea of contentment, not only because I was very much loved by them and the property staff but also because I lived in the countryside, an environment that I have loved ever since, and my days were a continuous adventure. From the coming of new strawberries, a fruit I still much love, to the long walks in the forest with the big old dog Galhito and one or two children of the servants, to rides on the donkey (a horse was too tall for me then), mine was a life of discovery and enchantment. Add to this the lavish gifts my grandparents used to present me with, and I could not have been a happier child, a little girl who enjoyed climbing high trees much more than being taken to an amusement park in the nearby town where my parents lived.

But it was the pine forest and the animals of the farm that had the most impact on me. Had I not experienced those early years I believe I would have been a different person. The enchantment, the bonds of love and the intimacy with the natural world remained with me throughout my life and the longing for those years is still poignant.

There were many chickens, turkeys, rabbits and other domestic animals in the property, living in almost total freedom, pecking grain, little worms and wild herbs wherever they wished in vast portions of pristine land. One of the great joys of my childhood was to witness the birth of little chicks, tiny clouds of fine, golden hair of great softness and delicacy touchingly tumbling around. I experienced those scenes as real miracles, something, which, many years later, I still think they really are!

And the pleasure became greatest every time I knew that a big mother turkey was hatching eggs for those were much rarer birds to hatch than the chicken. I would visit the mother-to-be several times during the day and go to bed thinking that I would check on how she was doing as soon as I got up.

One day I discovered that the maid who took care of the chickens and other animals on the farm would add dried broad beans to the turkey's special diet. But I did not know that the ingestion of broad beans had to be highly controlled. Thus, in one of those days of my adoration of the turkey, I searched for the broad beans, forced some of them down her throat, softly telling her that it would give her strength to hatch the babies.

To my horror and surprise the maid found the mother turkey dead a few hours later. My grandmother was puzzled and there was some stir about the incident since nobody knew why the turkey had died. I cried incessantly and wondered why it had happened. It was a great shock for me when they found out that the turkey's craw had burst because it was full of broad beans! I could not contain my horror and the feeling of guilt became so terrible that I thought I would also die of sadness. I kept repeating, "I killed the turkey; I killed it!" in the full flow of tears. Even my grandmother, who must have been very upset with the whole thing, showed no anger and tried, instead, to console me, albeit to no avail. It was a truly shocking experience, which I have never forgotten.

Since that time, death has meant loss … irreparable loss as I suppose it does for people in general. My infancy's first encounter with death was followed by others, perhaps less traumatic because I did not feel guilty, but they were always very poignant to me.

Firstly my paternal grandfather died, then two of my father's sisters followed while I was still a little child. Although I was spared the sight of their dead bodies, a secret carefully kept from me, I was left with an immense question about the meaning of such extraordinary events that I could not understand. I started to fear death; not my own but the death of those I dearly loved. And the person I loved most during those years of my childhood was undoubtedly my grandmother. The thought of her death was unbearable to me and I remember praying to God daily to let me die before her.

But I did not and her death, when I was in my early thirties, was one of the greatest sorrows of my life. She had been my love, my companion, my dearest friend and an adored role model since I was a very small girl. My grandmother was a tall, very beautiful and elegant lady, full of character and joie de vivre. I was an active, imaginative and rebellious child but she never fought my temperament. On the contrary, to a certain extent, she supported it in opposition to my parents who tried to change me. I literally adored her and thought I would not survive the pain of suddenly knowing that she would never again be there; that I would not see, hear or touch her, kiss and hug her again, an act that always brought me great joy. Her scent would stay with me for hours and I would remember it with delight throughout the day.

When she died, the immense sadness that overwhelmed me was followed by the terrible awareness of my impotence to change the situation and bring my grandmother back to me. I believe the pain and the impotence brought about by death can kill you.

The death of animals makes my heart bleed

The death of non-human animals has been a very traumatic aspect of my life ever since my early childhood. I still remember with horror the shrieks of panic of the pigs killed by the professionals on my grandparents' estate. At that time, in the 1950s, this was a common practice in the south of Portugal where I was born. There were men who specialised in this macabre job. They would go from farm to farm and perform it for a fee. I can no longer remember if the pigs started to screech when the men approached them or when they entered the property, and I wish I could remember because it would be an engaging thought. I have a vague idea that it was when they entered the rather long alley that led to the centre of the property, but I am not absolutely sure. What I do remember clearly is that I would start screaming even before the pigs did. I just could not bear it. I would get under the bed and cover my head with the pillows and try not to listen to the animals' desperate shrieks – which I can still hear. It literally made me sick. I went into a state of great distress, of shock almost. I dreaded the killing date months in advance to the point that I could not sleep long before it approached, thinking of the horror that was about to occur, and when it did happen it was so shocking that it has possibly affected my sensitivity forever. The whole thing was truly horrendous.

Another dreadful vision from my childhood of a very similar nature, was the terrible experience I once had when I was no more than five or so years old and I found the dead, skinned body of a lamb hanging from the ceiling, in a cellar, at my parents' home. At that time, mainly on special occasions when a lot of meat was consumed, lambs were killed in the garden, or the house estate, then prepared and kept in the refrigerator to be eaten at Easter and other celebratory events.

I lived in the Alentejo until I went to the University in Lisbon, and this was common practice then. I have no words to describe the horror and the shock I felt when I saw the body of the little animal hanging from the ceiling still dropping blood from its mouth. It had such a powerful impact on me that my parents had to take me to the doctor because I would not stop yelling and crying. Since that first terrible occasion, I begged my parents not to let that happen again at home, but there were other times when I found lambs hanging from the ceiling of the cellar and they again put me in the same state of shock with tears, trembling, dreadful nightmares and a feeling of enormous repulsion.

I must say that similar situations, although not so shocking in the sense that I do not react so intensely to them, still cause me great repugnance. For instance, on the road I cannot pass trucks loaded with pigs, sheep or cows on their way to the slaughterhouse without feeling terrible and nauseated, and tears spontaneously roll down my face. For instance, this morning I saw in a Spanish newspaper a shocking image taken at a popular country festival: two politicians, one local and the other visiting from England, toasting over a big platter with two roasted baby pigs joined together, their heads and open mouths raised above the surface of the tray in a grotesque grimace. The feeling of repulsion and disgust I suffer at such sights continues to be very powerful. And I cannot avoid judging the humans who commit these atrocities – unfortunately an overwhelming majority – and the culture, not to use the word civilization in such a barbaric context, which not only tolerates but finds these things normal and proper; perhaps even worthy.

Empathy with animals

Those painful childhood memories of animals bring to mind the issue of sensitivity or perhaps better said, empathy. It is true that I am a great lover of animals but I only realised recently, while randomly writing pieces for a future book, that I have had this deep empathy with non-human animals since I can remember. And in most of the cases, love was not involved because although I liked the pigs at my grandparents' farm, for example, we cannot say I loved them. Truthfully, I was even a little afraid of them.

As usual, I wonder if there is a reason for this to happen to me and not to so many other people. I will leave aside reasons such as karma and so on because I am neither versed on the subject nor minimally convinced of its pertinence. If there is a reason for this deep connection, which I would define as empathy, it is not immediately detectable, at least in my view.

Some years ago, in Italy, at a Conference in Turin where I lectured on ITC, somebody asked me at dinner why I was so fond of animals. I pondered the question for a little while and replied that through the proximity and non-verbal communication with non-human animals, I somehow found a deeper side of my own nature, which combines integration and primal innocence. It is as if I dive into the bottom of being where we are all one. I feel more complete through them, I told my neighbour, a medical doctor who seemed to understand my reason. Indeed, I feel no barrier nor a great difference between me and non-human animals. At least in things essential, such as love, care, perception and even death, we are all very similar.

The other day I got out of my garden gate and found a little mole that had probably been hit by a car or bitten by a cat and was about to die. The little shiny, blackish animal made a great impression on me. Its little front hands with well formed tiny fingers clasping in the air, the whole body arching in slight convulsions, foam coming out of its lovely pointed nose and, above all, the soft moaning, obviously caused by internal pains, highly disturbed me. I saw no difference between the agony of this tiny helpless creature and a human agony. Most people do, though, and it baffles me. As usual, tears came from my eyes and I wanted to help the little animal, perhaps move it into the shade or something, to make it more comfortable but I decided not to touch it and continued my walk praying for it to go fast. When I returned the little mole was dead. I was relieved and content that I had not disturbed it even more by moving or touching it.

Empathy with plants

Although not so powerful, I can feel almost similar sentiments towards plants. I have experienced several strange instances that point out to empathy with plants and I am puzzled by it. I'll give an example of this relationship.

I have been going to the same pharmacy in Vigo, the city near my house, for many years. And one day I noticed a miserable looking small anthurium in a flower pot standing in a corner. For a long time I didn't pay particular attention to it but one day, while waiting for my turn, I came close to the flowerpot and touched the soil in it. It was totally dry and hard. And, little as the plant was, the pot was still too small for it. When I approached the pot it gave me the sensation that the sick-looking little anthurium was choking. From then on, every time I visited the pharmacy to buy my vitamins and natural remedies, I would bring a bottle of water for the little plant. It was always dry because nobody had watered it in the meantime.

Maybe two years went by and I performed this routine every time I could. But on a very hot day in Summer I went again into the pharmacy and the little plant seemed to cry in anguish. It was all curled up and its fragile, completely desiccated leaves were becoming yellow all over. My heart shrunk, I got very angry, picked up the pot and took it home with me. The pharmacists looked at me in surprise, I told them the little plant was being mistreated there and I was going to take care of it. They said nothing.

I confess that I have great difficulty in coping with people who take care of the sick and recommend health treatments (as was the case at the pharmacy) but do not even notice the misery and sickness of a living being, which is under their care. I have found similar situations at some of the so-called spiritual centres, which I attended, for example in England. I remember being there and having a recurrent thought: "how can these people pretend to be spiritual and preach spirituality but allow a fragile, defenceless living being to die of thirst under their eyes?" I could not, and still cannot, understand such behaviour. How can such compartmentalising apply to sensitivity? However, this is a rather common behaviour in humans.

The little, fragile anthurium flourished at my house. I put it in the porch at the entrance of the house, a place where it would get some sun but also shade and no wind. Slowly it recovered the deep green of its leaves and, although emaciated by years of neglect, it seemed to rejoice in the open air, which I believe it experienced for the first time in its life. And one day a miracle happened! A tiny red flower, very small indeed because the plant had not been able to grow to its normal size and thus the flower was minute, bloomed in all its glory! It was very small but delicate, very well formed and one of the most beautiful petite flowers I had seen in my life! There was a very special quality about it, which I cannot explain. It was a minute flower of very harmonious proportions and vibrant as if it emanated light. The tiny red flower lasted a few days (I cannot remember how many) and then, suddenly, the whole plant died completely. It just disappeared in the soil of the pot. Nothing remained of it. I was sad and very puzzled. The whole story seemed so fantastic to me. To this day I wonder if the little anthurium just wanted to say thank you when it unexpectedly gave birth to what I called 'the most beautiful flower on earth' and then vanished forever without withering!

Naturally these experiences are subjective and have not the convincing power of a loud and clear ITC voice but they are very delicate and dear to my heart. I have experienced several of these wonderful happenings in my life.

In Lyon, where I lived for five years, an incredible incident took place and this was perhaps the most extraordinary of these marvelous events. I lived at Francheville, a wonderfully wooded residential area some 14 km from Lyon. The house was full of charm and emanated a scent of past and mystery. Built by an Irish lady, the beautiful thatched house looked as if it belonged to a fairy tale. It was surrounded by woods, which belonged to the property. I liked to go out and photograph flowers and trees. As usual, one morning I took my camera and walked through the woods to their limit. There were some shrubs with little white flowers and among those I spotted a lovely thistle covered with flowers. One of those had become a translucent white cloud of beauty, the ethereal tiny seeds flying in the air around it. Fine Spring sun's rays illuminated it in backlighting through the foliage of the forest. I was enthralled by the vision and eagerly pointed the camera at the beautiful flower sending fine hairs of light into the air. It looked like a dream. I was happy that I had managed to catch the airy little seeds surrounding the thistle flower, particularly because the lighting was very lovely. I turned back to go home but one moment later I thought I had not thanked the thistle for that special moment. For some reason the thought crossed my mind although I had never thanked a plant before. I returned to the thistle, put my hands around it and silently thanked it. At the very precise moment I did this I felt as if I was being raised in the air. Not very high, just some 15 or 20 cm, but raised in the air! I definitely did not feel the earth under my feet. An extraordinary sensation that I had never felt before and I have never felt subsequently. I was stunned and very moved and could not avoid thinking that for a brief moment I had levitated! What an extraordinary feeling! I never told anybody what had happened. This is the first time I have spoken about this extraordinary event, which was so special to me. My interest in photography had recently begun and I was not good at it but I used the photograph for the cover of *ITC Journal* n° 10, June 2002, and subtitled it with a sentence from my Rio do Tempo communicators: "Life is consciousness. All beings in the world are conscious".

My "Tuya"

I am convinced that my "tuya" (I am using the Spanish name), a tree of the genus Thuja Occidentalis, was the first plant to react to my feelings, if I may put it that way.

And at this very precise moment, while I write these lines, I feel like crying because I just found out something I didn't know and which I find very moving. Simply that the Thuja is also called arborvitae! Trying to confirm the translation of the word "tuya", I went to Google to research it and discovered that my "tuya" can also be called arborvitae or tree of life! I have had a fascination with the tree of life, which until now I thought was a generic designation for a symbolical tree, since my youth. And right now while I am writing, I discovered that the feeble tree of my garden that I cared for, because when I bought this house its roots were glued with cement, was the tree of life! I cannot get over it. But I will explain what happened from the beginning.

I bought this house in 1995 when I moved from my property near Lisbon to Galicia, Spain, due to my appointment as Consul General of Portugal. With the exception of a few trees, the garden was practically non-existent when I moved in. One of the very few trees (some five or six then) was this Thuja. It looked weak and lackluster, but I started watering it and wondered why it looked so frail.

One day, while doing something else, I knelt on the soil and picked up a twig, perhaps a small branch of thyme or rosemary or something else. When I did so I felt something hard under my fingers. I scratched the soil and, to my surprise, pieces of cement started to come out of the earth. I discovered, then, that the soil around the trunk of the thuja was surrounded by cement. This was also very strange because there was no reason for the cement to be there, the only place in the garden where I found it. Anyway, from that day on, I started to pick up the cement with my hands because I had not yet bought any tools for the garden. I watered the "tuya" daily and, to some extent, it recovered. I was happy because even if at that time I had no clue that trees might be sentient beings, I thought that I had done a good thing. In fact I only found out about J. Chandra Bose's scientific studies of plants (Bose, 1913, 1926 and other works) some years later, and, rather recently, I read Stephano Mancuso's Brilliant Green, (Mancuso and Viola, 2013) also about vegetable intelligence and sensitivity.

Back to my "tuya". When my dog 'Byron Lord Seta of Nisha' (one of my Doberman puppies) died I had him buried under the tree because it was almost in the centre of the garden. And, from then on, every time I passed in front of the "tuya", something that happened every morning when I went to my office, I looked at it and tears came to my eyes because I saw the stone with Seta's name engraved on it. One morning, while passing in front of the tree, I silently told it something like: "if only you could cover his tomb with your foliage!" and I don't know why I had this thought, something I had never thought of saying to any plant!

To my enormous surprise, two or three months later the branches of the "tuya" had grown in such a way that they covered Seta's grave and I could no longer see the tombstone. The most remarkable thing is that the "tuya" had not grown in height but in width; and its branches had grown in one direction only, not all around uniformly. They grew in such a manner that they totally covered Seta's tombstone from my sight. I did not know what to think, but in my inner being I dared believe that perhaps the tree had responded to my silent appeal.

As you can imagine, the thought seemed totally foolish to me because I found it impossible but, nevertheless, I developed a strong feeling for my "tuya", which, as I just found out today, December 11th 2018, is the tree of life. What a wonderful gift!

When I was assigned to my new destination as Consul General of Portugal to the city and region of Lyon, France, I was worried about the "tuya" and did not like the idea of leaving it behind. The tree looked beautiful then; it had grown luxuriant deep green foliage and a full breadth as never before. But I had to go and could not take it with me.

I got into the habit of asking how the "tuya" was doing every time I called the old couple who stayed in Galicia taking care of my house and garden. Surprisingly, one day they replied that it was not very well. I got worried and talked with my Rio do Tempo communicators about it. And, again to my great surprise, Rio do Tempo replied telepathically that my "tuya" had already passed into their world! I did not know what to think because, according to the people who were in Galicia, it was withering but it was alive.

I kept asking Rio do Tempo about the "tuya" and the same reply came through over and over again. At a certain point, because I had received the information from Rio do Tempo mentally, I doubted its correctness and thought it was my mind playing tricks. Furthermore, there was no doubt that the tree was apparently alive and this was also perplexing vis-à-vis Rio do Tempo's telepathic messages. I did not know what to think. I was confused.

In 2004 when I came back from Lyon, the "tuya" had dried up completely. I was so very sad but could do nothing. I left the skeleton of the tree erect in the little round garden around it for several years. There were also the graves of my beloved Doberman dogs, Byron Lord Seta and Barbara Lady. This small garden encircled by stones is located in the middle of the big garden. Many years later the dried "tuya" started to fall apart and, finally, I had it removed. But I think of my "tuya" often. Although I love all trees, this was perhaps the tree I loved the most.

I often think how very little we know about life, and also that we totally ignore what matters and what doesn't. Certainly, life is a mysterious event as David Fontana used to say!

Naturally I am aware of the fact that all I said about my tree can be interpreted from a normal point of view and many will say it was all a projection of my mind. But I very much doubt that a tree can add 60 or more centimeters of length to its feeble branches in two or three months! Experts will know but I have never seen it before.

Call it coincidence, which very probably it was, but the Spanish word "Tuya" – a name I had never heard before I was assigned to Galicia because I never studied Spanish – came into existence again at Marcello Bacci's centre in Grosseto, Italy, one evening when I was there and witnessed the DRV (Direct Radio Voices). At a certain point Bacci asked the communicators in Italian to speak with us, his guests of the evening, and immediately a masculine voice uttered in Spanish "... dicen que va más profundo que la tuya ardía". I was the only person there who spoke Spanish.

Since I could not find a translation that pleased me - I did not have a Spanish/English dictionary and Google translator was not available then - I wrongly translated the word "tuya" for African larch "... They say it goes deeper than the African larch burning" and I published the whole report on the experiment in the ITC Journal (See ITCJ 21, 2005, pp 19-28). The beginning of the sentence could not be properly understood. To this day I have not found out what this sentence means, although I believe it to be symbolical of some unknown concept, but perhaps the unclear beginning of the speech would provide an explanation. It could also be related to the "burning bush" of the Bible but I know no more... As it is, the significant fact for me is that Marcello Bacci's communicator mentioned a "tuya", the tree of life that I loved, and perhaps understood my sorrow.

6

THE ENIGMA REMAINS

The impossibility of understanding the next world

I have been receiving messages from the voices for the past 22 years. By now, I should be accustomed to the situation and find everything normal. To a certain extent I do, but I still cannot cope fully with the oddities created by these amazing contacts because they are many and disconcerting. Thus, the enigma remains.

The problem lies in the fact that we cannot comprehend, no matter how hard we try, concepts that deal with a different dimension in a timeless situation. Moreover, the prevailing values in that world, of which we can sometimes catch fleeting glimpses, are so very different from ours that the whole panorama becomes truly puzzling.

Consequently, the mystery that surrounds many concepts and issues put forward by ITC messages remains dense. I do not particularly like to offer explanations because I think there is always the possibility that I might unconsciously and involuntarily adulterate the information and, thus, give my readers a version that does not correspond to the communicators' intentions and ideas as I emphasised in an earlier chapter.

Interestingly, I found out that this point has also been confirmed by our partners from the next world. In Luxembourg they warned against erroneous interpretations of their messages and the same thing happened at Bacci's Centre.

My readers should be well aware of the fact that it is not always possible to interpret our communicators' speech as they perhaps intended. The whole business of understanding ITC messages fully is in itself a complex matter. The communicators often use metaphors, which are difficult to decipher; they can be read in different ways, all of which may be right and I can never guarantee that my interpretation is the right one.

Often, the communicators use symbolic or generic language. After David Fontana's death in October 2010, I have regularly asked about him. Although I received some specific replies (see *ITC Journal*, N° 39), every time I asked "Can David hear me?", the most frequent response was: "We hear everything" or "We always hear" and so on. Only on one occasion did I get a faint reply, which said "He hears" in the singular. Naturally, my questions and the communicators' replies are normally in Portuguese and I am translating them.

I know, because I have been told many times, that in order to be able to speak (through DRV) and send us messages, they need to work together as a team, thus, the use of the plural. Furthermore, as I always emphasise, their lives seem to be based on the Group-Soul structure and, consequently, this requirement is even more obvious. Nevertheless, my analytical, therefore limited, mind drives me to question and, to a certain extent, depending on the day and the mood I am in, to doubt if David can really hear me.

David's example, which applies to similar situations when I ask about certain people, illustrates an important point in ITC messages, which I believe needs to be discussed: what is implied by the difficulty in obtaining direct information from our communicators in reply to a direct question from us? From my comprehensive study of ITC literature, I am driven to think that at least one of the factors involved is the permission to convey to us a certain type of information even on trivial issues.

Also, from the literature, we can easily reach the conclusion that only the Technician and, to a certain extent, Swejen Salter gave direct, comprehensive replies and explanations to their human counterparts, the Luxembourg operators, and to those who participated in the sessions. Professor Ernst Senkowski, physicist, was one of the scientists who closely followed the development of the contacts in Luxembourg. He became Swejen Salter's preferred interlocutor. In her physical world she had also been a physicist and, through Maggy Harsch's computer, she used to send him long computer texts about complex scientific and metaphysical issues (Senkowski, 1995).

In the case of Adolf Homes, the communications were mainly in the form of spontaneous computer texts. I recall Professor Senkowski telling me that he used to write questions on a piece of paper at his house in Mainz and often the replies would appear on Adolf Homes' computer screen at Rivenich without the operator's intervention.

Friedrich Jürgenson and Konstantin Raudive were pioneers and came at the beginning of EVP but even they received replies to some of their questions but not others. At Marcello Bacci's center in Grosseto the same thing happened. For instance, the communicators rarely identified themselves except when a deceased child or a family member, spoke to their deceased relatives (a marked feature of Bacci's electronic voices).

In my case, Carlos de Almeida (see Cardoso, 2010) used to reply to most of my questions. However, on the afternoon of September 2nd, 1998, when he spoke uninterruptedly with me for well over one hour and I asked him all the metaphysical questions that still preoccupy me, his long, very loud replies could not be fully understood. His words seemed to be truncated; there were phonemes and syllables missing and, overall, they could not be understood. This was one of the saddest moments of my ITC experience. I was so keen on receiving information on existential issues, which I deem fundamental from those who are more advanced than us and, having received the information but not being able to understand it, was even more frustrating.

Because Carlos de Almeida replied to every single question I put to him on that afternoon!

Maybe the Technician's statement in Luxembourg would apply to this unfortunate situation, which I regret to this day. The high entity asserted:

"What you receive from our reality are mostly distorted radio signals, which for this reason are frequently misinterpreted." (Senkowski, 1995, F-38.11.2 Transentity Techniker).

Incidents such as the one above are not rare in the life of those who work in the mindboggling field of ITC.

One of the things we definitely learn is that it is indispensable to be patient and to accept what life brings us. I have to confess that, in general, I am not a particularly patient person but my ITC work compels me to be so. Either I cope with it and wait for what is to come unwearyingly or I give up all hope of obtaining good results.

Marcello Bacci's communicators told us that they always endeavour to come through to us but patience [from our side] is required. Said one of Bacci's communicators in reply to a question on how to improve the quality of the voices:

> We try the most possible to insert ourselves, it is necessary patience." Bacci commented on the advice: "This statement given to our Roman friend and collaborator will certainly be useful also for all who despair or endeavour to the establishment of a bridge with the voices; in fact psychophony is chiefly constancy and patience. (Bacci, 1991, p. 82).

Indeed, this is true and anyone interested in the extraordinary ITC adventure must be aware of it before starting on his or her own exploration.

The meaning of life

One of the most pressing issues humans have conceived is certainly the quest for the truth, a truth which would explain everything. I believe we could replace the word 'Truth' for 'Ultimate Reality' or 'God' and it would carry the same meaning.

I have a friend in Australia, a subscriber to the *ITC Journal*, who pursues the meaning of life through the noble quest of dismantling the many small "truths", while searching for the one "Truth". He writes to me often expressing his interest and sharing his thoughts on this topic. He would very much like me to try to obtain valuable information from my communicators about this important topic.

His queries focus mainly on the points: "Does life have a meaning?" and "What is the meaning of life?" I certainly share his interest but, to my dissatisfaction, I feel impotent to help him in this quest. According to my friend, all of mankind's small 'truths' – religions, movements, ideologies, etc., instead of driving us closer to the 'Truth' separate us from it. I think he means that because they falsely claim that their small truths are the universal 'Truth' then, consequently, they 'do more wrong than good' as the saying goes. I certainly share this view but avoid discussing the issue because I have no definitive answer.

But at Adolf Homes', the high level entities some of non-human origin, were more detailed. And I quote from the Italian translation of Prof Senkowski' s compilation of Homes' computer messages:

> Anything related to the psyche consists of open fields; therefore there is neither truth nor non truth. Each dimension knows different concepts and truths. The truth of the divine light is neither one nor two. It is simply as it is. Christianity, as it has been established, is a distorted aspect of the fundamental truth because it connects the good with the bad while neither one nor the other might occur.

The knowledge of wise beings tends continuously to the hypothesis that there is no ultimate truth.

Beware of men who tell you the truth. The latter is contained only in the original information. The probability line that you take for the truth is subtler than the thread of a cobweb. Focus more on probability and you will come closer to the truth. Also, we and many others are still very far from the truth. Before reaching the spirit of truth everything undergoes transformation.

In love, in the devotion for the veracity, we approach the greatness and the inconceivability of God. The truth of the love for others will bear every junk information. Only after your metamorphosis [death] will you be closer to the light and to the truth." (See Senkowski, 1999, p. 130).

I must recognise that I find it impossible to know with certainty what 'The Truth', or 'Ultimate Reality', is. The approach to this important question may be varied but I deem it impossible to find ultimate reality and the universal purpose and meaning of life; not least because such meaning would imply a different path for each one of us, humans, without forgetting our companions – the other animals, plants and minerals. Perhaps the meaning of life, if it exists, might not be universal; it might be personal.

If I had to describe in a few words how I understand the meaning of life, I would say that the meaning of life is simply to experience life. And that the experience of each one of us – humans, animals, vegetables and minerals – albeit different, is equally useful and important because it is God in movement, God in evolution as I prefer to put it – rather than some entity; that there are no negative or positive experiences, just experiences.

Interestingly, just a couple of days ago I found not only Homes' message on love but the following in one of the works about Bacci's communications:

The risen Spirit will be a real surprise, your substance will let itself be transfigured without losing its dimension of diversity, and there it will find a way, it will be a different way, where it will live forever.

No, the truth is not something absolutely acquired, it is a set of data, which is assembled gradually; your experience always implies a change in the commitment to grow spiritually you too, call it over time to live it, so you must never leave it. (Pagnotta, 1992, p. 132).

Allegedly, the anonymous feminine voice belonged, as the majority of Bacci's communicators, to a highly developed deceased human being and I find she pronounced words of much wisdom. This is certainly a great approach to the concept of the truth – a non-universal truth.

Nevertheless, I suppose each one of my readers would be interested in finding 'The Truth', the only one. However, finding the Truth is a complex matter.

Firstly, how can 'The Truth' be found through somebody's agency, even an entity from the next dimension? Said like this, 'The Truth' appears like a grand, objective revelation which, if found, would become immediately recognised and accepted by everybody and, obviously, would replace all the small 'truths' proclaimed as 'The Truth'.

A thousand questions come to my mind when I ponder this issue. A major one regards the existence of 'The Truth'. Does 'The Truth' exist? The concept of the 'Universal Truth' has necessarily to imply wholeness; it should be a revelation valid for everybody of whatever kind. Is that possible in our world if not in others? I do not think so ... Thus, a relative truth valid only for some, let's say for humans, would not be 'The Truth'. Unless we argue that the non-human beings, which, together with us, populate this planet are of no value; hence they should not be considered in this philosophical discussion. But who are we to make such a statement? Do we consider ourselves God? What right do we have to put forward such a proposition? In my opinion none at all and, consequently, I deliberately leave the question of 'The Truth', to which I have no satisfactory answer, open.

Besides, I gladly accept the information transmitted by high entities to Adolf Homes as the most valid path in this quest: "Each dimension knows different concepts and truths … ", and "The knowledge of wise beings tends continuously to the hypothesis that there is no ultimate truth." Perhaps we could add that each being knows different concepts and truths. I believe we could.

I had the privilege of meeting Masanobu Fukuoka, the revered sage, author of fundamental works on life and its ways, with whom I stayed for few days in the south of Japan. During our wonderful meetings and conversations, Fukuoka Sensei advocated that the purpose of life was lying down on the grass and falling asleep under the sun as well as scattering seeds on the soil without interfering in the least with nature's ways, respecting what we call weeds and allowing them to grow, together with the other plants we need for food or health (Fukuoka, 1987). I feel that he is basically in the right direction.

7

THE TOIL

ITC voices are hard labour

ITC operators must be prepared to work and to work hard if they aim to receive meaningful communications from the next dimension of life. This is not an easy task, as anyone who gets into this exciting journey will soon realise. I have spoken about it at length in previous works (see Cardoso, 2010 and the *ITC Journal* 2000-2017) and I am sure any ITC operator will corroborate my words. The temperament to endure long lapses of time without any results and to try many different ways to attain the best results once the voices have manifested, is essential. But, above all, it is imperative never to become discouraged even if the voices are not forthcoming.

From their side those who identify themselves as our loved ones strive to come through, to communicate and, once the contact is established, they try by all possible means to give us personal identification about themselves because they know this is such an important condition to convince us of their existence. Sometimes they are reprimanded by other voices for providing identification (see my CD 'Electronic Voices' at www.itcjournal.org). Alternatively, and although there are exceptions, the voices that finally offer a name in reply to the operator's repeated appeals, seem to do it reluctantly and only after being pressured, perhaps because permission to speak with us is an important concession and they fear losing it if they identify themselves.

Personal identification, among other issues, needs special permission. And I will explain what happened in my own experimentation that corroborated my statement. At the beginning of the DRV when my own father started to speak with me, I recorded a conversation in which a masculine voice, apparently my father's, announces clearly and loudly "I am João Cardoso!" This is immediately followed by another voice that interrupts and tells him "You don't have to say that; only Rio do Tempo!" Therefore, he should not say his name, only the station's name.

However, later on and even now, my father identifies himself practically every time the voices speak. "I am João Cardoso", "It's João Cardoso speaking", or "It is your father, João Cardoso, speaking" etc., have become recurrent sentences whenever the communicators are able to make it. It does seem that my father has now the necessary permission to identify himself at will.

We just do not know how things really are in the next world and we cannot do much about it except speculate. But I find the differences described above interesting and indicative of a state of full consciousness of the entities behind the voices.

Let me clarify, one of the consequences of disobeying the prevailing rule of not yielding personal identification seems to be the cessation of the contacts or, at any rate, a suspension of the latter. This has happened in Brazil with Oscar D' Argonnel's telephone calls as documented in his marvelous little book (*Argonnel*, 1925), which I described in previous works (Cardoso 2010, 2017). It is reported to have happened at Marcello Bacci's Centre in Grosseto, too. For instance, on page 132 of Silvana Pagnotta's book on Bacci's communications, *Risveglio alla Vita* (1992), the author states that Bacci wanted to know who was speaking but a feminine voice did not acquiesce to his curiosity and reproached him: "It is useless to wonder who these people are. You [Bacci] worry about these things instead, above all because you have already met them" (literal translation from the Italian).

The role of the earth operator

A ll I said in previous chapters does not prevent me from questioning the devotion I have for my ITC work, something that has conditioned my life to a point I never deemed possible.

The voices are not only charming conversations with the deceased; I believe that for our communicators who produce them they involve (if we could count by our time), thousands of hours of what they call "our work"; i.e., sentences repeated over and over again, continuously, in an apparent exercise of learning how "to modulate the radio waves with thought", as they say, to produce human language. Undoubtedly, this work must require enormous concentration from our communicators. Rio do Tempo told me several times, usually at the end of a long DRV session particularly when the voices could not be properly understood, "We [they] are very tired". When I inquired if they were tired because of the concentration effort required to produce the voices, they confirmed, "That's correct".

I have recorded hundreds of such sessions, the ones they call "our work", something the remarkable Italian experimenter Gabriella Alvisi also experienced. In her books, e.g. *Le Voci dei Viventi di Ieri* (1976), she explains what she calls the "diction exercises" carried out by her deceased daughter who explained when she questioned her about the lowness of her and other communicators' voices: "Mama, I am learning!"

But the earth operator also experiences this labour for a number of reasons. One of the main problems is that often the electronic voices are not clear and fully intelligible. There are exceptions, of course, as happened with the Luxembourg communications at the end of the 1980s but, overall, audio ITC may also consist of hundreds and thousands of indistinct messages, some of them not clear at all, which cannot be understood except for a few words.

In my case, when this happens, the latter are frequently "mortos" (dead), "Rio do Tempo", "Cardoso", "É o pai" (It is your father), "Somos nós" (It is us), "A voz já passou" (The voice has already passed), "É o Só" (It's Só) and a few more. The identifiable words are normally followed by a long chain of speech from which bits and pieces seem to be missing or is distorted to the point of making it incomprehensible, always with the same end-result, that is, the impossibility of understanding the whole of the message.

These fairly common occurrences can truly make us despair because we know they are important messages or even just messages that we would like to decipher since they come from our loved ones, or from advanced entities, and we are unable to understand them. Naturally, particularly at the beginning of our experiments, this drives us to listen and listen to what cannot be understood, resulting in terrible fatigue, which sometimes can make us wish we could disappear from the face of the Earth! The frustration and the feeling of discouragement, particularly if we get many of such communications, may make us ponder the sense of it all.

Jürgenson puts across eloquently what I have experienced, and experience, in moments of frustration. With the kind permission of the Jürgenson Foundation (no longer extant), I quote from the English translation of one his books:

> Often I came close to losing my patience, and the work seemed unending and hopeless. My love for art was still as strong as before, and I asked myself with a heavy heart, if I was justified to give up my painting, a creative occupation to which I had once devoted my whole life.
>
> The fact that I gave up painting just at a time when I was starting to savour my success did not bother me greatly. However, the thought of Pompeii pained me as I had been entrusted there with a unique task that was to have been accomplished in the spring. Instead, I was

sitting here in Stockholm in front of a jigsaw puzzle, struggling with frustration in trying to assemble a clear picture from all the countless fragments.

And yet, never before in my life had a subject grabbed and fascinated me as deeply, as these mystical contacts floating around the ether. In the sober light of everyday common sense, the whole thing seemed like a fantastic fairytale or some crazy eccentricity. But fairytales and castles in the clouds are not in demand in our times of rough reality.

Reason and intellect rightfully demand facts, touchable, measurable things that our senses can comprehend and explore. A stone, a drop of water, an invisible atom, even an abstract mathematical formula can be understood by a human mind, no matter how different they are. Rationality is our guideline, and at the same time, it is the border that may not be crossed. For sure, my tapes and radio contacts with the inhabitants of an invisible world could have been considered illusions or a fairytale, if not for the existence of the tape recordings.

To my great happiness and relief, these touchable real tapes, a gift from beings out of the ether, lay before me. Their content, in word and sound, could be heard and understood by everyone who wasn't deaf or retarded.

Despite all difficulties and mountainous obstacles, I was filled with silent gratitude; yes, I perceived it as an act of grace, for in these tapes lay a hidden wonder with undeniable proof of the reality of another world, another sphere of existence. Everything was new and original surpassing by far in significance all of my personal wishes and expectations.

That, which had happened here, which repeated itself daily and slowly gained a clear outline, possessed the explosive power of pure truth based on facts.

It was the truth, the reality, which was possibly called for to tear the curtain from the hereafter into a thousand pieces and, at the same time, to bridge over the abyss between here and there. In no way could this be called an idle sensation. The one and only thing that mattered was the fact that I was entrusted with the great and difficult task to push ahead with the construction of this bridge. (Jürgenson, 2004).

The concept of the 'Bridge' mentioned by Jürgenson has been frequently put across by the communicators, as I discussed in previous books (Cardoso 2010, 2017). It is the bridge that allows this incredible interchange between the two worlds. Over fifty years later, I corroborate, word by word, statement by statement, from my own personal experience, the remarks that the great pioneer of the electronic voices offered.

A DRV sentence that I received from my communicators years ago illustrates well the labour, which the ITC operator on the earth must be prepared to bear: "Podes ajudar a comunicação, significa o teu trabalho" (literal translation: you may help the communication, it means your work).

This work may involve many different aspects. I described above one of the most complex phases but there are others. I have spoken extensively about the necessary approach to the work with the voices in other books (see Cardoso 2010, ibid). Thus, in short, I will say that it is a work for life. Self-criticism, honesty, commitment, persistency, patience and trust are fundamental.

Friedrich Jürgenson, based on his own experience, had already offered:

Those who are seriously interested in taking part in the bridge building here and there will also need to devote much time, patience and effort because positive results cannot be expected without personal engagement. First of all – and this is the essential point – it all depends exclusively on the motives on which we base our desire to initiate contacts with those who have died" (Jürgenson, 2004, p. 164).

The electronic communications with the dead are indeed the outcome of a common endeavour by the entities, namely scientists in the next dimension, and our own. The joint effort developed in two dimensions brings about the wonder of the direct communication and exchange of information between beings of this and the next plane of existence. An indescribable joy!

We must be aware of the difficulties involved

Notwithstanding the fact that acoustic delusions (the so-called pareidolia) might happen and be dangerous because they create false hopes, particularly in people deeply affected by grief, there are other circumstances which should be taken into consideration before labeling everything as pareidolia, as ill-intentioned or misinformed critics and observers of the voices often do.

The nuances are many; there may be very soft voices in the recording that only the ear of an experienced listener or acoustic expert can detect. At this point, I challenge sceptics about the reasons why this problem happens; I mean why normal people cannot hear what a proficient experimenter or sound technician can. Indeed, there exists a psychological mechanism called pattern recognition, which may well apply to audio information. And while the negative face of this mechanism is pareidolia, or false pattern recognition, the positive one is that the experienced ITC operator – in general a person of excellent hearing ability and thousands of hours of training in listening – can detect meaningful sounds and real verbal content in audios that a normal, inexperienced listener would classify as noise only. Therefore, just because a majority of people cannot hear what the competent experimenter avows he can, it does not mean that what the experimenter claims is untrue. The final decision should be taken by one, or several, experts in sound recognition. A complex task but a necessary one if somebody wants to debunk a reliable, reputable ITC operator, as often happens.

Another unfortunate outcome when the voices are too soft or blurred is that several people hear different things in the same recording. There may be, in that case, several interpretations of the same audio.

Overall the main reasons for this are:

- the poor quality of the voices as described above;
- the insufficient hearing proficiency of the listener or listeners.

Moreover, it is very important that the listener or listeners are native speakers of the language of the recording or, at least, highly proficient in it. Preferably, they should also be linguistically educated. It is wrong, for instance, that a native English speaker listens to, and assesses recordings in Swedish, Polish, Italian or any other language in which he is not fluent. I have seen many such cases with the consequent biased and incorrect evaluation of the audios. The regrettably famous debunking of Dr Raudive perpetrated by David Ellis is based chiefly on the erroneous interpretations of native English speakers – Ellis and a group of students – of voices in idioms of which they did not have any knowledge (Ellis, D., 1978).

Professor Hans Bender, one of the greatest parapsychologists of the twentieth century, was conscientious and meticulous to the point of having the best sound technicians of Germany analyse and evaluate Friedrich Jürgenson's audios obtained during the controlled experiments carried out with the Swedish pioneer of the electronic voices under his direction (see *ITC Journal* 40, 2011, pp. 61-78).

Hence, the complexity of serious ITC work is obvious and anybody interested in getting into this marvelous adventure should be aware of it. Our communicators' as well as the earth ITC operator's endeavours should be duly valued.

8

THE POWER OF LOVE

It's all about love!

'The power of love' is a worn out expression misused by everybody, mainly in the New Age literature, which I particularly dislike, but it is one that conveys the circumstances that drove me into, and keeps me in, the quest and labour ITC represents.

It all started in the summer of 1993 at a pleasant beach in the south of Portugal. A friend had invited me to accompany her and her family to the cottage they rented in the fishing village of Vila Nova de Milfontes. After much hesitation, I finally accepted but thought it would be to no avail because I could barely speak. I felt so tired, so sad and depressed that words are not enough to describe the anguish that I carried in my heart. I had just lost the love of my life, my beloved dog Surya. I thought I would never again be able to live a normal life. It took me at least two years to be able to interact with other people in a normal way. The pain remains even today.

For many years, I could not pronounce his name and, even less, write about him. However, today, although tears come to my eyes, I make the effort because I want to convey to my readers what I think was my first telepathic thought, the only one for many years until some time ago.

I was on the beach distraught beyond description, hiding my tears from my friends and walked alone into the sea. At that moment a sudden and completely unexpected thought flashed inside my head with complete clarity and brilliance. It said, "When you die, you will laugh!" I was so surprised because clearly that was not of my own creation. It hit me twice and it addressed me, I mean the thought addressed me; it spoke to me, albeit silently, "When you die ... " I did not know what to think and although I never forgot this experience, I dismissed it and continued to be miserable for several years. This happened in July, or perhaps in August. Surya had left after a terrible, prolonged agony on April 15.

Years later when I started my ITC work and achieved results, Rio do Tempo brought me news of Surya and his beloved mate, my lovely Nisha. I thought that perhaps it was all connected. It occurred to me that Rio do Tempo had already spoken to me on that beach in the summer of 1993 when I felt like dying.

Years later, as I recounted in one of my books, I started to receive regular telepathic information from Rio do Tempo. So perhaps this strange thought was indeed the beginning.

Love is a strange and powerful emotion. Antoine de Saint Exupéry's little prince in love with his rose, very well illustrates the personal sacrifices and pains, which love normally demands.

From my side I believe that my love for Surya triggered my profound interest in ITC and was certainly at the origin of my love and dedication to many other dogs, indeed to all dogs, including hundreds of little, abandoned, abused creatures that I recovered and saved from horrible deaths very often at the cost of my own rest, peace of mind and the savings of a well-paid professional life.

It all went into the construction and financing of "Abrigo", the shelter for abandoned animals, which I founded and built on my property near Lisbon where it still functions today. Although I have loved animals for as long as I can remember, after Surya my love for them grew to extraordinary levels. It is as if each one of them brings me a soft breeze, a caress. My love for Surya continues to grow every day through them.

I dream of Preto

At the end of the 1994, or beginning of 1995, while I was working in Galicia as Consul-General of Portugal, I had a very beautiful and strange dream. One night I dreamt I was flying with a big black dog. His hair was compactly curled. We were flying above fields and country houses, with him on my right side. Suddenly, he turned his snout to me (I had not yet seen his face, only his body) and it was my beautiful Surya's snout, the beautiful face of a proud and elegant Doberman! I was very impressed by the dream because the dog's body was not my Surya's nor the body of any other dog I knew.

I had already rescued some thirty abandoned dogs that were living at my farm near Lisbon, where I also lived before moving to Vigo. However, I had never seen this black dog's heavy body with very tightly curled hair. In addition, although Surya was also black, only the snout was Surya's; nothing else matched.

One or two months later (I cannot recall the exact time) while driving around Vigo exploring some of the local beaches, I saw one big dog lying down in a ditch by the side of the road. I stopped the car to check on him and saw that he was a big, heavy black dog that could not get up. I parked the car as near as possible, and with difficulty lifted him into the car. I took him to my farm in Lisbon, had him checked by the veterinarian (he had a serious liver condition). I called him Preto (Black in Portuguese). He stayed there and lived for a few years. In the meantime, I recalled the dream I had had of a black, heavy dog with tightly curled hair and Surya's face that was flying with me. Then I realised that the dog's body and hair were exactly like Preto's! I was fascinated and interpreted the dream as a message of support from my beautiful, beloved Surya. It made me very happy.

At the time, one could find miserable, sick, abandoned dogs almost everywhere in this region of Spain – on the roads, on street corners in villages, no matter where – there would be hungry and sick dogs that nobody cared for, that people normally disliked and kicked or, at best, were completely insensitive to their plight.

When, finally, I moved to Vigo after finding a house with a suitable garden, my two Doberman 'puppies', Barbara Lady of Nisha and Byron Lord Seta of Nisha (I always called them puppies although they were already six-year old dogs) came with me. The other two, Blackie and Michi, had already died. The thirty abandoned dogs I had recovered in the period in-between, stayed in what would become Abrigo, Associação de Protecção à Fauna e à Flora, my property near Lisbon.

The role of the heart

Jürgenson, to whom I always return because I feel so close to him, especially after having visited his beautiful estate at Nysund of serene beauty and harmony, one of the most beautiful places I have seen in my life spent all over the world (see *ITC Journal* 34), wrote: "The dead speak the language of the heart" (Jürgenson, 2004). He expresses it better than I could and, in this regard, I recall an anonymous communicator who intervened suddenly via the DRV, on one of the occasions I was in Grosseto at Marcello Bacci's Centre: "What does your heart tell you?" This is a typical example of the way the voices communicate most of the time. Bacci's communicator was not replying to anybody, addressing anybody in particular or even referring to anything that we had said during the DRV recording session; but he left a message, and an important one, in my opinion.

Coming back to Antoine de Saint-Exupéry's *The Little Prince*, I truly find that this is the most spiritual book I have read. In my view, each paragraph is a teaching of high ethical value. One of its most interesting characters, the fox, told the little prince, "One sees clearly only with the heart. Anything essential is invisible to the eyes" and like everything else in this precious little book, it reveals wisdom and truth at a very deep level. A similar thing happens with the voices. Your heart tells you they are who they say they are and this is all that matters from a subjective point of view. Of course, I know it is not sufficient for the sceptics or those who are not familiar with the subject, or for science, but that is another issue. Personally, it is all that matters because your heart does not deceive you.

Actually, the most obvious characteristic of the anomalous voices is their genuineness. Jürgenson admirably characterised the electronic voices with the sentence above: "The dead speak the language of the heart" and I will add that the rule of the heart appears to be the law in the next dimension of life. The rule of the heart and the rule of truth prevail in that mysterious world that baffles us all, me as much as anyone else.

Speaking about laws I must tell my readers that, according to our communicators, there are strict laws in that next world from where the electronic voices seem to emanate. Indeed, and very interestingly, the same information was already conveyed to the first person on record to receive telephone calls from the Beyond, the Portuguese-Brazilian Oscar d' Argonnel (D' Argonnel, 1925), whom I have mentioned. On page 21 the next world communicator speaking to the author, his partner on the Earth, informs "We have strict laws here and today I am not allowed to communicate with her [the recipient's wife]"; and on page 45 "... I have already told you that we here can do nothing without higher consent". Every time I open this marvelous little book, I cannot avoid being fascinated by the similarity of the information received in our world in the 1920s and the information we obtain today through ITC.

I said at the beginning that this would be a book on my perceptions and deep feelings. Hence, I do not feel compelled to prove anything. I did that in my first book, which referred to a compact disc with samples of the voices that can be found on my website www.itcjournal.org

It is the voice of love

Love seems to be the key to our communicators' contacts with us. A very powerful masculine voice posted on the *ITC Journal* website clearly says: "Mortos! É a voz do amor!" (The dead! It is the voice of love!).[4] Moreover, on several other occasions they shouted, "Bela, we speak through love!" (translation). Or just "We speak through love" many, many times. "This is the voice of effort" is another designation my communicators frequently give to their work as I mentioned above. It seems that love and effort go together as they normally do, although I believe they do not mean love in the sense we understand it in this world. Theirs goes far beyond ours.

The high entities that communicated with Adolf Homes via computer texts have been even more explicit:

> Love is the root of everything that exists. Life is love. Love is life forever, a consolation for men. Love is the purest form of energy. It is a unique centre of information. Love is to be found in information. The real meaning of information is still difficult for you to understand. Love and concord are important concepts. Love is a supradimensional concept, which for you is only roughly correct. In love and again in love is the fundamental law that presides over all that exists. The Natural Law is love.

> Love is a multidimensional aspect of the divine power. All that exists is embedded in the big unconceivable love of the Great Spirit in the eternal river of the whole being. Only love is able to surmount space and any time. To know love opens all doors. To recognise love in all things is the key to the Omnipotence whose love is far greater than we can imagine.

---

4   See: http://www.itcjournal.org/?p=4690

> In the love for yourselves as well as for All-That-Exists,
> we find all the realisations of the Great Spirit. If you
> love every being as yourself, you are worthy of the Great
> Spirit and Creation. The love of the Omnipotence is in
> all things (Senkowski, 1999, p. 53, German original).

The description of "Love" by Adolf Homes' communicators
is several pages long. Thus, I have translated only the most
significant parts because the message is similar throughout.

It is understandable that love must be the key to these
extremely difficult to achieve communications, and perhaps
that is the reason for the bliss that a dialogue with the voices
brings to the heart and mind of the ITC operator, even when
we cannot identify those who speak. Naturally, being human
in a still underdeveloped state of being, we exult when we
speak with our beloved deceased ones but, in general, the joy
encompasses all voices. The magnificent re-encounter with
those who have left our world cannot be expressed in words
alone, which are always so lacking and limited. Only emotions
can convey it but these, too, by their very nature, cannot be
defined effectively through language.

My main communicator, Carlos de Almeida, said once
from Rio do Tempo Station: "É convocar o amor sem género.
É p'ra essa gente humilde, é convocar o amor, panaceia do
mundo, seria bonito, não é?" (Literal translation: It's to call
upon love without gender. It's for humble people, it's to call
upon love, panacea of the world; it would be beautiful, won't
it?).[5] When Carlos de Almeida uttered, "… to call upon love
without gender" I figured he meant something similar to what
I am trying to convey, i.e. love without restrictions, without
distinctions, without conditions, love for everybody and
everything – mineral, vegetable, animal and human. Love for
rivers, oceans, mountains, stars, love for all life. This must be
pure, overpowering love, not love that is conditioned to "you
love me and I will love you" or "you benefit me, I will love you"

---

[5] See: http://www.itcjournal.org/?p=4690

or "you are part of me or of my family, my group and so on and I will love you" to give trivial examples of what I mean. The Portuguese word 'género' means kind, species, and gender; therefore, I suppose my interpretation is acceptable.

Indeed, when all vanity that had been embedded in my life vanished, only love remained and the awesome joy of knowing that those I loved and had died lived in an invisible place, somewhere I could not penetrate but from where I could hear about them or, sometimes, directly from them. This was all that mattered. It is a feeling incomparable to anything one can imagine.

I remember thinking that even if I had to live a life of misery until the end of my days, it would have been worth it. Years ago, when I addressed my deceased father and asked if all the difficulties he had lived through in this world were justified in view of his new life, a voice replied with simple words "It was all worth it!". This is how I felt.

At the core of my reaction, surely incomprehensible for many because I had so much to lose in terms of the values of our world, was love. What one feels for these mysterious communicators and not only those who identify themselves as our loved ones, is love that goes far beyond what we normally call love – as I tried to explain above. We do not see them, cannot touch them, know about them or who they are, as we can here on the Earth regarding the people we know or even people we don't know … but we trust them and what they tell us because these voices carry the resonance of truth.

There is also the chatting, the informal conversations between the communicators that we can sometimes hear, the remarks they address to us or make about us, which prove conclusively their knowledge and understanding of who we are. One of the beautiful chants I have received from Rio do Tempo says "*Nós somos vós, somos todos pobres homens…*" (We are you; we are all poor humans…) See CD Electronic Voices.[6]

I have noticed that sometimes the communicators seem to know more about my inner feelings than I consciously do,

---

[6]   http://www.itcjournal.org/?p=4621

and this is something that strikes me as odd. It is as if they were part of me at a very deep level. In a way, I feel they are simultaneously extrinsic and intrinsic to me. This is really a strange feeling, which does not diminish the strong conviction that the voices are from whom they say they are.

I wrote this chapter long before I thoroughly read Belline's *La troisième oreille*, thus, I was thrilled to have just found in this work a situation similar to that which I have just recounted. On April 10, 1971, Belline tells his deceased son: "Michel, sometimes I have the impression of speaking to myself and listening to my own responses" (p.116). In addition, on page 117-118, Belline says, "... Michel, I have asked myself if our dialogue was not a projection of my unconscious. Michel, you do not reply. Can you hear me? Then the son, Michel, utters, "I can hear you. What to reply? I am your son. You are me and I am you! We form a unity; we emit waves that we perceive. Isn't it natural?"

In my case these impressions are not so intense because the voices that reply to me are loud, powerful, masculine or feminine but completely different from my own and therefore, I know that I am not speaking to myself; yet, I feel them at the deepest level of my inner self. A strange feeling! Beautiful but strange.

My paternal grandfather comes back!

I will give a striking example of the effect that the electronic contacts can have on us. I have always been very fond of my father to whom I feel very close. But I hardly knew my paternal grandfather because he died when I was six-years old. I knew of him and was interested in him mainly through the love I had for my father who was deeply attached to his own father.

Since my ITC work started but particularly later when my communicators told me my paternal grandfather was very involved, I developed a deep affection for him, although I can hardly remember him. I feel deeply moved in a way I never deemed possible when I hear a voice utter "It's your grandfather Cardoso".

I adored my maternal grandparents with whom I lived for the most part of my childhood and youth, and that grandfather, Frederico Mourato, was really the only grandfather I loved because not only he was lovely but also because he was the only one I knew. For me he was 'my grandfather'. I have listened to a masculine voice say during a DRV contact "It's Mourato speaking!" which made me very happy but these days when my other grandfather speaks or I hear his name being spoken, I am equally moved, as if I have found another wonderful grandfather who also seems to be instrumental in my ITC work. The love and affection for my paternal grandfather developed only because of the ITC communications I receive. Before that, although I regretted it, he was just a vague memory.

In a certain way, the love I have for my father has also grown. I witness his (and his group's) enormous efforts to make the voices possible, his struggle to provide personal identification whenever the voices come through and I often cry.

Throughout his life, my father was an indefatigable white-collar worker. Even beyond his professional life at the Ministry of Finance, he did not leave a task undone whatever it might be, and no effort seemed too much for him when he had a job to do. He was thoroughly reliable and honest. Like his father, he was a man of honour and principles. Maybe it is because I know him and, therefore, I can judge better, but I get the impression that not only his main traits of character persist but also, it is because of them that he is able to communicate with me so frequently. This is just a strong personal impression, though.

Bonds of love develop with our unknown communicators

Even when we do not recognise the communicators by the names they sometimes reveal to us, we still become much attached to them as if we had known them for a long time; as if they were close friends. I wonder why this feeling of trust and affection develops. I was never inclined to doubt my communicators, perhaps because I never detected any malice in their words and because I never found any wrong or deceitful information in their messages. Some irony, perhaps, when they make fun of my little manias and idiosyncrasies. The entities from the next world always speak bluntly and show a great sense of humour.

From our side, we should speak with our soul, too; pretense will get us nowhere: not only because it is ethically wrong, but also because they know our thoughts.

The feeling of attachment to my main communicators is so deep that once, while talking with Professor David Fontana about Rio do Tempo, I remarked, "How extraordinary that I know my Group-Soul while still in this world!" Truly, this is what I feel.

The bridge

The famous 'bridge' about which so much has been written in ITC literature, starting with Friedrich Jürgenson, could also intervene. Said Carlos de Almeida, many years ago, through the DRV: "I have already put the bridge!" What is this bridge, which, presumably, is indispensable for more advanced contacts such as the DRV? It is not a physical bridge at least not one made of the visible matter. Could it be a telepathic bridge? Once more, we do not know but it is a possibility. If this were the case, emotions could be transmitted and received across it. Friedrich Jürgenson offered on the important issue of the communication bridge, "First of all – and this is the essential point – it all depends exclusively on the motives on which we base our desire to initiate contact with those who have died.

If we wish to ultimately banish the suffocating fear connected with death, we have to become conscious of our ancient inner distortions in which our thinking and feeling have become ensnared in a vicious circle of time, space and causality. We all need to go through a kind of twilight of the gods and demons to rediscover the path to the human heart after the shattering of our illusions" (Jürgenson, 2004, p. 164).

Years later, the deceased Jürgenson posited via Adolf Homes' computer: "Each [one] of your and of our thoughts has its own electromagnetic reality that does not get lost outside of the time structure." (Cardoso, 2017, p. 48). From my side, Filipe from Rio do Tempo Station uttered via the DRV, "Always think of our world; whoever thinks of our world reduces the distances". Jürgenson's and Filipe's statements use different words but I believe they describe a similar situation.

Does this young girl want to dance the waltz?

Once one of my beloved communicators, Carlos de Almeida, told me affectionately and jokingly, "Esta menina quer dançar a valsa?" (Does this young girl want to dance the waltz?). "Menina" in Portuguese is a gentle, affectionate expression that can be used in relation to anybody of the feminine gender, from one-day old to the end of her life, although its true meaning is a young girl. It is a nice compliment considering that I must have been around 50 at the time ... On another occasion, he uttered "Tu és Anabela Cardoso ou moça que eu não conheço?" (Are you Anabela Cardoso or a young woman I do not know?). The friendliness of such comments is clear, and, although we only listen to the voices, strangely we do feel the emotions they transmit.

I reckon several legitimate questions might arise about this issue. We know, because the communicators have told us, that the voices are synthesised, at least the DRV. How is it, then, that we can perceive emotions through a synthetic voice? It is true that some voices, albeit rarely, sound like the voices of the same people they are purported to belong to but, overall, the voices do not resemble the human voices we knew. Thus, perhaps they resonate in us because we are part of the same group, of the same big family of the soul and are united by everlasting bonds. I think it could very well be so. Rio do Tempo has told me "The soul connections are never lost". I spoke of the Group-Soul in a previous chapter and wrote about it extensively in other works thus, I will not get into the matter in detail here (See Cardoso 2010, 2017).

Some very special communicators

There are communicators who, at our request, identify themselves with names we had never heard before and cannot recall knowing. One of those was Joan Colbert who, years ago, at the beginning of my receiving the DRV, seemed to lead to many contacts. One day I asked, "Who is speaking?" and a feminine voice replied in Portuguese "Fala Joan Colbert ..." (It's Joan Colbert speaking ...) followed by a whisper that I could not understand. I cannot recall a Joan Colbert in my life, so I presume I did not know her from life here on the Earth. The same voice used to speak a lot and speak very well, thus she must have been an experienced communicator. I became very attached to the feminine figure who intermediated the contacts and responded clearly and loudly to my questions.

One summer, two English friends who were also interested in ITC visited me. I asked them to listen to some DRV recordings, which were partially in English. As a matter of curiosity, I asked them to listen to Joan Colbert and they did so intently. I asked if they could understand the whisper next to the name and, after careful listening, the two ladies confirmed, but she says "past"! I listened again attentively and I agreed. Therefore, the full reply to my question was "Fala Joan Colbert (pause) past". I trust we can interpret that the woman's name in this world had been Joan Colbert. In my opinion, this was a very interesting reply for several reasons. The main one being that names are not so important in their new life as in our world. It will probably have to do with the Group-Soul, the unimportance of the ego and so on. Their reply to my question, "who did all this work to establish contact with me, here at my house?" was: "All of us! It was all of us!"

A Portuguese friend of mine, Maria dos Anjos Antunes, who, after becoming acquainted with ITC through my work, started to experiment on her own, once heard the following statement from communicators who had also identified themselves as being from Rio do Tempo Station, "We are all fused!" No other expression could convey better what I muse on the unity of the Group-Soul.

There were other communicators besides Carlos de Almeida and Joan Colbert, to whom I became much attached. One of them was Filipe, already mentioned several times. He spoke at length and beautifully about his "power of infinity" that he described as a "colour", and other things. He brought me news of my beloved Surya and I was forever grateful to him. After that unexpectedly long talk, he would occasionally, albeit rarely, just utter, "It's Filipe, how are you?" and an ocean of joy engulfed my heart.

Another communicator, whom I do not recall knowing, replied one day when I asked: Rio do Tempo, is it you, Rio do Tempo? "Oh Bela, I'm coming!" Next, a masculine voice immediately responded to my customary question about who was speaking with a clear, "It's Pedro Roque!" (uttered twice) followed by "It's Pedro Roque speaking". He called me Bela and only my family members call me Bela but I cannot remember him.

Will unknown affinities of the soul bind us to the unknown beings who speak with us? I believe it is a strong possibility and one that accounts for what I have told. I certainly know that the Group-Soul – an assembly of beings from different kingdoms of Nature intimately bonded beyond the physical – is not All-That-Exists but it is perhaps a big step towards achieving the whole.

Our ITC contacts are something our current paradigm defines as impossible but we should remember that, fortunately, paradigms change and what was once the 'impossible' suddenly becomes a fait accompli. The history of humankind is full of such examples. Many people in the past were murdered and a great number were defamed because they announced what was to come and shook up the established paradigm. However, they were right and what they postulated did eventually happen.

9

THE VOICES CHANGED MY LIFE

The communicators know all our thoughts

Our friends and beloved communicators are aware of the conflict produced in our minds because of their contacts. As I have told my readers, at the beginning of the DRV I was permanently baffled. On one occasion, a feminine voice suddenly told me during a DRV session: "Just pretend we are all equal!". She went straight to the point. That is, I am not able to face the electronic voices as a natural happening, and obviously she could feel my doubts. As they say, "We know all your thoughts" However, even if I react as I have described at length above due to my upbringing and education, I defy anybody not familiar with the subject to listen to voices that address him or her calling out their names directly from a radio, and tell me how they reacted after that. I am sure they did not experience the occurrence as a normal event.

F. Jürgenson replied to one of the journalists who interviewed him on the voice phenomenon:

Question 6: Why did the dead opt for such a technically prosaic method as the tape recorder? Would not a living medium be more impressive, as has been the case until now?

Answer: No matter how prosaic and sober a mechanical tape recorder may seem, its construction excludes that it is subject to any personal errors, imaginings, wishes and desires.

A tape recorder will function a hundred percent objectively; it registers in a purely automatic fashion those electromagnetic impulses that come its way, either via the microphone or via a radio receiver connected directly to the tape recorder. However, in the case of microphone recordings, other reception possibilities also seem to exist, namely under certain conditions that have not yet been entirely determined, there are other parts of the tape recorder that can be used as access channels. The supposition lies close that the communicators and singers on the other side can also make use of other parts of the instrument instead of just the microphone. As already mentioned, there is the justifiable hope that this problem can be solved soon with the assistance of scientists.

There is no doubt that a mechanical tape recorder cannot be compared to any [human] medium because of its absolute objectivity. We know, besides, that genuine and dependable Spiritist mediums are extremely rare; certainly this is the case in Europe. No matter how talented and basically honest a medium might be, he or she cannot completely eliminate subjectivity. Thus, for instance, no medium can differentiate with absolute certainty whether the impulses arriving from its subconscious originate from the dead or from those present, because the borders in this case are fluid.

I also consider it a disadvantage when participants in spirit-séances unavoidably become to a certain point dependent on the medium. Such a dependence relationship can easily paralyse personal initiative and independent research." (Jürgenson, ibid, p. 101-102).

I would add that to seek survival evidence and direct contact with the dead on its own, through technical means, is undoubtedly a much more laborious and difficult task than to consult with a medium who can be reliable and genuine or not. And if results come true, the direct, personal contact with his or her deceased loved ones is infinitely more rewarding and meaningful. At Bacci's, parents of deceased youngsters told me that hearing his son or daughter's name come from Bacci's radio addressing them, had not only transformed their lives entirely but also that nothing else could have convinced them of the youngsters' survival. They unanimously declared that this realisation brought them unparalleled joy.

At the beginning of receiving my own DRVs I had to deliberately assume an attitude of detachment and attempt to achieve a blank state of mind, free from judgment, to be able to work calmly with the voices – digitise them, classify them, transcribe them and so on. Currently, I am so much more accustomed to speaking with the voices that I no longer need to become detached from what is, in our view, the absurdity of the situation as was previously the case.

Unexpectedly, one day in March 1998, they changed my life forever in a dramatic way.

To begin with, I was a career diplomat, an ambitious, demanding and highly regarded profession, in which it is very hard to succeed. I was among the first small group of thirteen women allowed into the diplomatic service and the first woman Consul in the history of Portugal. It was a landmark appointment. In the USA where I was posted as Consul of Portugal to Rhode Island, my first diplomatic assignment, I was awarded an *Honoris Causa* doctorate, mainly for this reason.

I was a professional of high repute, diligent, smart and, according to my colleagues and superiors, intelligent and successful. They said I was pretty attractive, too. As a matter of fact, I suppose I had all the requisites to become a very successful Ambassador. But it all happened during my stay in Lyon as Consul-General.

One day, a couple of Lisbon newspapers published full-page stories about my talks with the dead: "The Consul-General in Lyon: Passport to the other world!" was the main headline right across the newspaper's centre pages. From then on the telephone at my office did not stop ringing and the Secretary General of the Ministry of Foreign Affairs wanted to speak with me personally. I knew there was not much I could argue in my defence and decided to let it all go. This was something I had wanted to do for some time – to devote myself entirely to ITC research and the publication of what I had experienced and learned from these wonderful communications.

I asked for leave of absence and returned to Galicia, the beautiful Northwestern region of Spain where I had bought a house overlooking the Atlantic Ocean and the bay of Vigo. I had not done it before for financial reasons but, after this incident, I knew my career at such a conservative institution as the Foreign Ministry of Portugal would be in jeopardy. My request was greeted with open arms for they would get rid of someone who had become a highly embarrassing diplomat. And although I felt a little worried because I feared financial difficulties, I was finally free!

I am, and have always been, a very independent person. I never regretted having left the diplomatic service because what I was doing seemed so much more important than what I had been doing until then. My new job was an unexpected joy, a gift from the universe, perhaps, that I found on my path without knowing why. It was also the most difficult work I had ever done, but the most gratifying as well.

Thus, all of a sudden, everything I had fought for, namely my career with all its implications, no longer meant anything to me. The taste for the beautiful, luxurious receptions as the many I attended at the New Otani Hotel in Tokyo, where I had been Chargé d'Affaires, the reunions with the Crown Prince of Japan, later the Emperor and recently retired, the dinners with the maharanis and maharajas in New Delhi, the encounters with the Heads of State in other countries, plus the opulence that money affords us, the cook and the driver, the expensive cars and clothes, the flattery, which people in prominent positions normally receive ... they all dissipated like smoke, which indeed they were. A new era had started in my life.

When dogs speak

Although I am an agnostic, a free thinker not observant of social or traditional customs and models, I still suffer from involuntary bias regarding the communications from the dead.

In general I am not prone to prejudice and thought I was free of it, at least in most issues in life. But the voices have made me realise how deeply undetected prejudice can be ingrained in our mental universe. Prejudice is perhaps the most damaging of all thinking patterns, and all the more so because in many cases we are not aware of it.

What I offered about prejudice with regards to the voices of the dead in general, applies very neatly to the messages that some of us receive from deceased animals other than humans (let us not forget that we are all animals), although not particularly to me because I have no anthropocentric tendencies and avoid anthropocentric views, in spite of the fact that we live in a (bad) world constructed by, for, and around humans.

I have received more than one DRV in which a voice seems to encourage and guide my dog Nisha to speak with me. Once, a masculine voice from Rio do Tempo station told me, "Nisha learned how to speak through the radio and she wants to speak with you!" In this statement two situations become clear – firstly that speaking through a radio requires a learning process and secondly that in her new world, Nisha has the freedom to do what she wishes, apparently with the permission, which we are told is a basic requisite to contact our world. Since then, Nisha has spoken on a number of occasions and identified herself to me. The conversation she had with me years ago is a beacon in my life and my ITC work and still moves me to tears all this time later.

Só speaks and he speaks well

Só was an abandoned little dog that I found staggering across a blazing road under a 40°C sun, a real living skeleton in which every single bone was visible. He was also ill. I picked him up and brought him first to my mother's house until I could prepare accommodation for him in the country house where I lived with my Doberman dogs. Naturally, he had to stay alone in a separate enclosure and so I called him Só ('Alone' in English). The deceased Só has spoken many times throughout the years.

Só's story is an interesting event in my ITC contacts. I am an animal lover and certainly a dog lover. A very deep bond connects me with dogs. It all started with my beloved dog Surya whom I loved as I have never loved anyone else in my life – as I have stated in a previous chapter. This love extended to Nisha, my female Doberman, and four of their puppies who lived with me until the end of their days. This love is still present in every dog I rescue and even in every dog I meet.

Só was one of the many dogs I saved. I loved him, of course, and felt special compassion for him but I must say that I did not love him more than the many other abandoned dogs I have recovered. However, it was Só who, among all the other deceased dogs that have crossed my life, took the lead and is active in most of the contacts apparently originating from my family. In many cases he even seems to be the one who facilitates the contacts with my dear family members. Often the voices begin by saying: "It is Só" other times, "It's Só with mother", It's Só with father" or "I am Só, I am a dog, I live" and so on. Once Rio do Tempo told me about him: "In our world Só is a dog chief" (literal translation of the Portuguese).

Certainly this did not happen because he was, or is, my favourite dog but perhaps because of his own capabilities. Or possibly because he suffered so much in this world and we are told that suffering is an extremely important asset in the next world and is essential for spiritual evolution. Maybe it was sufficient credit to enable him to become a leader among the communicators. Is there, at last, cosmic justice in that mysterious dimension? I don't know but I wholeheartedly wish it to be true.

Although they always puzzle me, I have given up on understanding the ways of the next world. After all, "It is a world very similar to ours but with very different values" (See Cardoso, 2010). And, while theirs is a world "very similar to ours but much more beautiful" as the communicators keep reminding us, perhaps this similarity applies only to the physical aspect of it while the mental and spiritual facets are different. As things stand we can only guess.

I am perfectly aware of the fact that many of my readers will find the communications, which I received from some of my dogs – namely voices that utter loudly: "Sou o Só, sou um 'perro', penso!" (I am Só, I am a dog, I think!)[7] or "É a Nisha" (It is Nisha), "Sou a Nisha!" (I am Nisha!) and so on – very odd to say the least.[8]

Other abandoned dogs that I rescued also spoke via the DRV and gave their names.

Very recently, while I go through the manuscript of this book, the name of my gentle, beloved female cat, Corsi, who died at the end of 2018 when she was over eighteen years old, appeared recorded during the EVP experiments, which I organised with a small group of people during the pandemic quarantine. I brought Corsi from Corsica where I had found her, abandoned, extremely mistreated and scared, to my house

---

[7] My communicators frequently use the Spanish word "perro" to speak about a dog. I don't know the reason for this but I suppose it could be related to the stronger sonority and, therefore, better intelligibility of "perro" in regard to "cão", the Portuguese word, which sounds muffled.

[8] See an example of Nisha's talk at: http://www.itcjournal. org/?p=4690

in Lyon and later to this house in Vigo, where I currently live. The feminine, clear little voice made me very happy because Corsi's death was a terrible blow to me. She had never been able to rid herself of the scars caused by her horrible life in Corsica where she was persecuted by a drug addict who systematically terrified and tortured her. I had an immense tenderness and love for my gentle Corsi, the sweetest of all cats, and to hear her name clearly uttered in an EVP experiment brought solace to my heart.

I know that some will not believe me; nevertheless what I say is absolutely true and accurate. Those messages can be understood by anyone who is not hard of hearing; however, I suspect that, even so, prejudice will prevent many from believing what they hear.

In addition to the apparent absurdity of the dead speaking through the loudspeaker of a radio, the content of their communications reinforces this impression. It is not only the fact that some voices identify themselves, as in my case, as deceased dogs and cats, but other unexpected details such as, for instance, the good-humored chatter, which the voices sometimes produce, also emerge. And, naturally, we have enormous difficulty in accepting it because, after all, they are supposed to be dead!

The voices are often humorous and joyful and say simple things that take us aback, teasing the operator playfully. On the whole, they sound cheerful and speak in such a casual manner that we could easily think the dramatic, final episode we call death had never happened. I recall one of Rio do Tempo's DRV sessions when one of the voices that spoke that evening uttered: "Se tu soubesses" and a little later, "A morte é tão bonita!" (If only you knew, death is so beautiful!). At this point another voice interrupted to say "Certo!" (Right!) and the first voice continued: "É feia é no espaço!" (It is only ugly in space!).

At Bacci's a voice also stated: "... Death is precious! I know what I say, if death can be called that fullness of life!" (Pagnotta, 1992, p. 25)

But here in this world, we expect the dead – even if we accept the fact that they did not really die but just transitioned into another dimension – to be grim and solemn. This is a natural reaction on our part, albeit one that applies mostly to the western world. It is related to our social, cultural and traditional religious models, even for those who follow no religion. Our reaction is based upon our mental patterns, the ones we absorb from birth and observe around us throughout our lives.

Our communicators must learn how to speak

Let me give you an example. Even those who accept the fact that the dead do not really die, have great difficulty in accepting that dogs, horses and other non-human animals can express themselves in human language. Consequently, they think only humans are able, or entitled, to communicate from the next dimension of life. It sometimes never occurs to them that the human language is the only one understood by us, humans, and in a world much more advanced and much richer in possibilities than ours, non-human animals may be able to learn how to express their feelings in human language, too. After all, deceased humans must also learn how to speak via ITC. And, it seems, not only via ITC. In his book *Life after Death: Living Proof,* Tom Harrison wrote from the careful log he kept of his mother's materialisation sessions:

> 7th Sept. 1946 ... Douglas Hildred then whistled through the trumpet but was unable to speak. Sunrise explained he would have to learn to speak, as he passed over as a baby. (He did gradually learn to speak and we then had many interesting conversations with him ... ") (Harrison, 2008, p. 107).

We will get back to Tom Harrison later in this book.

I have several electronic voices, both EVP and DRV, which say (EVP): "Sei parlare!" (I know how to speak) in Portuguese and Italian, and in at least one of the DRVs that I remember, a feminine voice tells somebody: "You know [how to speak], so you must speak!" (translation).

Our ITC communicators have told us that we hear their thoughts and this is very likely what happens. Once I asked my communicators if they told us what they wanted to say or if they said what they thought. Their reply was very interesting: "We say all that we think" (translation). Perhaps this is also the reason why several ITC operators, myself included, report listening to a number of mixed voices in the background of DRV recordings. These could very well be the thoughts of the group of beings involved in the communication process.

After all, literally speaking, we cannot hear their own voices because they no longer have vocal organs. Dead humans do not possess the vocal organs necessary to produce vocal speech sounds; however, through ITC, we do hear sounds, which clearly resemble human voices, and I emphasise the word 'resemble'. In the majority of cases, though, they do not even resemble the voice of the communicating person when he or she was alive. High entities stated in Luxembourg that ITC voices are synthesised and also that it is extremely difficult to reproduce a voice identical to the voice of a certain person while they were on the earth (Locher and Harsch, 1989, French ed. 1995, p. 146).

I once asked my own Rio do Tempo communicators how they produced their voices and their clear reply was: "You can be sure that we masquerade, they do us a sonogram" (see CD 'Electronic Voices'). Albeit in the typical enigmatic language used by the electronic voices, what better confirmation of the information received in Luxembourg? "Masquerade" (this was the exact word in Portuguese they used) could be interpreted that the voices are not really theirs; and a sonogram could be the metaphor used to describe the process of creating the voices. This is just an interpretation, of course; there may well be others.

Cultural habits and traditions influence our thinking patterns

Many years ago when I lived near Lisbon, I was visited by a gentle and relatively well-educated man who came to speak with me about some work at the shelter for abandoned dogs that I was building there. We talked about dogs versus humans and I gave him my opinion that, in general, the latter are less generous, reliable and loving than the former and asked him what he thought and how he refuted my view. I will never forget that this kind, fairly cultured man pondered for a while and offered a single reason: "But they don't go to the bathroom!"

However, not everybody reacts this way. I was assigned to New Delhi, India, where I lived for almost three years. One member of my house staff, Ram Prasad Godyal, came with me to Japan and later his son joined him in Portugal when I finished my assignment to Tokyo and returned to Lisbon. I find it very interesting that the boy, who then stayed with me for some eight years, and, consequently worked at my house in Spain, when I started the ITC work, accepted the existence of the voices easily and with very little emotion. For him the whole thing was an entirely natural event, while for me and my two friends it was exactly the opposite. A good example of how cultural differences and heritage affects us.

10

THE PASSAGE: A MYSTERIOUS CONCEPT

The voices frequently mention the "passage", an intriguing concept that I find very interesting. I have recorded in my studio and, most importantly, under strictly controlled conditions at the Department of Telecommunications of the Technical University of Vigo, many EVPs and DRVs in which the word "Passagem" (Passage) can be clearly heard (See *Neuroquantology*, 2012). Normally, the anomalous talking in which we find the word seems to be part of a conversation between the communicators who utter comments in sequence such as: "Não há passagem" (There is no passage), "A gente dá passagem" (We will grant passage), and similar examples. Remarkably, in the latter case, immediately after the voice uttered, "we will grant passage", all the voices of that afternoon became clearer and much louder. I believe the "granting [of the] passage" was the reason for the voices' improvement.

Recently, during a DRV session at my studio, a masculine voice uttered "A voz passou o espaço!" (literal translation: The voice passed [through] space!). I find this expression extremely interesting because other voices, on other occasions, have joyfully announced "We're already in space!" or simply "We're in space!". Considering that the voices used to say – particularly when I began receiving the DRVs – things like, "Your grandma went to get a voice", or "I have no voice" or "Oh, my voice is going!" and so on, I wonder if "the voice" is something 'produced' for the communications with us and, in a certain way, detached from our dear communicators, i.e. a kind of tool they use to communicate with us. This would make the sentence "The voice passed [through] space!" a little more comprehensible, because perhaps it is easier for them to pass [through our] space than the voices they use.

I am speculating, of course, but it is a possibility, otherwise why would they repeat innumerable times for the last several years, usually at the end of the DRV contacts: "The voice has already passed" or "The voice passed" instead of saying "We have already passed"? It is true that the language used by the electronic voices is sometimes vague, something perfectly understandable given the circumstances, among which is the scarcity of energy that they must fight, but the affirmation that "[my] grandmother went to get a voice", for example, truly astounded me when I heard it all those years ago. It gave me the impression that the voices were comparable to a device, which the communicators used to make contact with us and the idea truly shocked me because we cannot separate our own voices from ourselves inasmuch as we are not able to separate ourselves from our own body.

I must confess that not being absolutely sure of anything with regard to the next world is very frustrating for me and this is perhaps when faith plays a role: neither religious faith nor faith in a god or gods, but trust in those we hear and cannot see, and in what they tell us.

Examining the sentences above, we could also mull over the meaning of space. What does space mean to them when they talk? Is it the universe, our physical space or mental space or what? Another question with no certain reply:

"Há passagem" (There is passage), "Já passaste!" (You have already passed through), etc. are comments I have recorded frequently in past years. Other operators have recorded similar statements. The "passage" itself seems to be the most important requirement for a good and clear contact. But again, what exactly does this passage mean? Like everything else in this area, we have no way of finding out for sure because our communicators do not always reply directly to a question, or there is no opportunity to ask them or, as in my case, I never thought of asking them at the time when my conversations with Carlos de Almeida were fluid and frequent, and he would reply to practically all of my questions.

We could speculate – and I think this is a strong possibility – that the "passage" often mentioned by the communicators refers to the passage between dimensions, as in the sentence "The voice passed [through] space", or simply, as they often say, "A voz já passou" (The voice has already passed).

A few years ago, I recorded a very interesting DRV sequence in which the voices mentioned the "passage" loudly and clearly. The speech of excellent quality was carried out by two main interacting voices, one feminine and one masculine. I published a report about this unexpected occurrence in the *ITC Journal*, issue 41, August 2011, pp. 46-49, and called it "Sou o Tom!" (I am Tom!). A transcription follows:

"SOU O TOM!

Anabela Cardoso

On Thursday, March 31st 2011, during one of Rio doTempo's customary DRV speech practising sessions at my house, which I have described elsewhere, the most unexpected voice came through. It was a loud, fast and utterly clear voice that almost shouted in Portuguese, "Sou o Tom!" (I am Tom!).

That evening, Rio do Tempo's contact lasted for over 30 minutes. It had started with one of the usual feminine voices which, following Friedrich Jürgenson's classification of the clearest voices, I tend to attribute to Rio do Tempo's 'speakers'. Firstly the voice announced: "Oh Bela, o Luís!" (Hi Bela, Luís!). Bela, as most of our readers already know, is my pet name used only by very close family members and Luís was my deceased brother's name. The voices talked a lot that evening saying things like, translated from the Portuguese: "It's your mother", "It's your father", "It is the voice, it's the contact of Rio do Tempo", "Hi Bela, Luís!" which they repeated several times... and so on. Every now and then, during these working sessions, the voices repeat sentences several times in an obvious exercise of speech, as is also mentioned by other operators (e.g., Alvisi, 1976, Schäfer, 1992).

The powerful masculine voice uttered "Sou o Tom!" at 0,0dB, my audio software's top measurement. It was immediately followed by one of the clear feminine voices that remarked, also in Portuguese: "Ele tem voz, até está igual" (He has voice, it is even alike); it paused and continued: "Ele teve um passagem, ele teve vantagem" (He had a passage, he had advantage). Some 30 seconds later, the same masculine voice intruded again into the feminine recitation of words and announced "Sou o Tom!" now at -4, 0 dB. The feminine voice immediately followed with: "Ele tem voz, passar!" (He has voice, pass!). The voice that vigorously affirms "Sou o Tom!" and the feminine voice that obviously comments on "Sou o Tom", as described above, has been heard by several dozen people of different nationalities; there was no discrepancy about the content. The linguistic content of "Sou o Tom!" is unmistakable even for those who do not understand Portuguese.

Naturally, I was puzzled by this voice and wondered who this Tom might be since I don't know anybody among my friends or acquaintances, anywhere in the world, called Tom. And then it occurred to me that it could be Tom Harrison, Ann's husband. The more I thought about it the more sense it made to me. In fact, the content of the feminine voice's statements could entirely apply to him. The voice said "He had a passage, he had advantage"; knowing that the economy of language together with the symbolic use of words seem to be one of the main characteristics of ITC voices in general, I thought [a good passage] was implicit in "he had a passage". And this made perfect sense! Certainly Tom had a good passage because, as the voice said, "he had advantage". And his advantage could very well have come from the teachings and experiences, which he inherited from the period when he lived with his mother and aunt.

If it really was Tom Harrison, the only puzzle remaining was why he spoke in Portuguese, a language of which he had no knowledge. I know and speak English perfectly well, so I suppose it was not because he was addressing me. Was it because he was, at the moment he spoke through the DRV, working with the Portuguese Group at Rio do Tempo Station? It could be but of course we cannot be sure.

(As I mentioned earlier), one of my very first DRV voices, a clear feminine voice that closely followed my experimentation for a long time, identified herself as Joan Colbert. She used to speak and reply to me mostly in Portuguese but, sometimes, also in English. I mean she would say a few words in Portuguese and continue with a sentence in English, all perfectly clear.

I suppose the most important lesson to learn from the remarkable voice that vigorously stated "Sou o Tom!" is that we really do not understand much of what is going on in the subtle levels of reality. My beloved Doberman dog Nisha was born in India and we used to speak to her in English. However, the little human voice that through the DRV identified herself as Nisha, and said a few words, spoke in Portuguese, not in English. And when I, in English, requested a confirmation from the little voice asking: "Is it you mummy?" she again clearly replied in Portuguese: "Sim!" (See: CD Electronic Voices). Also, on one of the occasions Professor David Fontana spoke with Rio do Tempo in English, the first reaction of the voices came in Portuguese, "Nós falamos português" (We speak Portuguese) they said, and then proceeded in English.

If we fully assume that one of the ITC lessons is the fact that the intellect does not seem to play any appreciable role in the communication process, while emotions certainly do play a major role, and if we recognise that we know so very little about these essential aspects, not only of the next world but also of this world, Tom's beautiful affirmation of existence and identity would have served a great purpose.

Notes

1. It appears very interesting that the voice clearly used "um" instead of the grammatically correct "uma" because "passagem" is feminine in Portuguese. The wrong use of the articles is typical of some foreigners speaking Portuguese, predominantly English nationals, because the English language has no male or feminine forms.

2. 20/9/2011. I have now listened to the CD that Ann Harrison sent me and listened to Tom's natural voice. At direct listening, both voices are not dissimilar at all. The anomalous voice is much faster, as commonly happens, and is more vigorous, but the timbre seems compatible, considering the recording quality of the 1950s. This is just an informal assessment without any technical implications because real voice comparison must be done by an accredited forensic expert.[9]

I have mentioned Tom Harrison's sessions above but not in detail. Let me briefly explain who Tom Harrison was and why the words of Rio do Tempo's voices apply so well to him. Tom's mother, Minnie Harrison, was a famous medium who produced awesome physical phenomena including the materialisation of full body ectoplasm that could be photographed as it appeared and was subsequently published in her son's book, *Life after Death: Living Proof* (See bibliography).

The encounters with the deceased took place on Saturday evenings at the home of Tom's parents. The little group of deceased people would sit down with the living family members, talk with them and bring them astounding apports as gifts. Tom's Aunt Agg was the famous professional medium Mrs. Abbott who demonstrated at the Queen's Hall in London in the Thirties.

To my knowledge, the very incredible phenomena produced through the physical mediumship of Minnie Harrison and the

---

[9] I will gladly send the audio clip containing the DRV passages above mentioned to interested readers. It will be cost-free but I need an E-mail address."

spiritual guidance of Aunt Agg from the next world were flawless and never suspected of fraud by the experts who analysed the evidence provided through the many actual photographs, which were also considered to be genuine.

Do we need faith?

As I suggested above, although not in the religious sense of the word, I believe that faith, or trust, plays a big role in these splendid contacts. Because we deeply feel (and this is the right word to express what I wish to say) that the communicators are who they say they are; therefore, we trust what they tell us, although the information we receive is truly astounding.

The deceased speaking through radios? Telling us stories of another world? Another dimension beyond time in another space? Saying that all beings transit into this "pure world" after physical death? And supra-human entities, such as the Technician or ABX Juno, telling us they are of a different nature and that plants communicate with humans and animals in a world of grace, "a world very similar to our world" but very different in many aspects, and so on, and so on. Let's acknowledge that it sounds much more like science fiction than reality.

My own communicators put it clearly in one of their long DRV contacts. At a certain point the message says literally this: "We returned, we came back, we came, you had faith in [Rio do] Tempo!" (translation from the Portuguese). The utterances were repeated several times. (A few excerpts of this communication are published in my CD Electronic Voices, Example 25, Voltamos!).

I will explain briefly why Rio do Tempo insisted in avowing that they had returned because I "had faith in Tempo". A few years ago, I did not receive any voices – DRV or EVPs – for a period of two years. Nevertheless, I never stopped turning my radios on and doing my normal EVP experimentation on the scheduled days. I would not receive any voices and even less replies but I would still stay in my studio and talk to my communicators on the scheduled days, twice or three times a week as I currently do. I would not go anywhere on those evenings and, as usual, at the request of my communicators I would turn off my desktop computer, as I still do today, and carry out my EVP experimentation.

Frankly, at the end of two years I thought the voices had definitely stopped as has happened to other operators. But I kept trying and performed the same routine as when the voices were forthcoming. I believe this is the reason why they started that evening's contact by joyfully proclaiming: "We came back, we came, you had faith in Tempo!" It is true that I have faith in Tempo and this is the same as saying that I have faith in love, for love is the force that drives me. Love for the deceased whom I deeply loved on this earth and love for the unknown entities that I feel so close to, who endeavour to communicate with us, poor and disoriented humans, to bring us "the good news of grace", as my dear friend François Brune used to call ITC.

Just listening to a minor part of the content of the most significant ITC messages is sufficient to switch off the vast majority of people, independently of their intellectual, cultural or social level. Information of such kind just cannot be. And what 'cannot be' does not exist for some people. It is as simple as this: the human brain is not prepared to accept concepts, which thoroughly contradict the prevailing paradigm.

Thus, we have two alternatives – either we accept what our communicators tell us with all the consequences this choice implies, or we dismiss the whole thing as rubbish (as the majority of people do). It is up to us, dear reader.

If we choose the first alternative, as I did, we need to be coherent. What we cannot honestly do is to wish that the communicators tell us what we would like to hear them say and I will give an example of what I mean. In a seminar somewhere in the USA, which I watched on YouTube, I heard a participant say: "Well, this time she [I] went too far!", in a remark about my second book, *Electronic Contact with the Dead, What Do the Voices Tell Us?* Nevertheless, this was an unfair observation because there is nothing in that book of my own judgment. It all came from the communicators and, on the whole, not even from my own communicators. And the communicators said what they said. No more and no less. I just reproduced it.

But if we accept the first alternative, we will soon realise that the world we live in turns out to be a farce because we understand it is merely something that we, humans, created but have lost track of its spurious nature. This is when we need to make 'tabula rasa' (a clean slate) of all our concepts and models and recognise that what they taught us was the rebuff of the cosmic truth that we will all reach one day. Life in our world becomes painful because we question everything and we find out that from our new thinking perspective, almost everything we took for granted is wrong. Our consciousness has expanded.

Once you, dear reader, have fully accepted your new mental structure brought about by our communicators' information, I urge you to look at all other living beings, our companions on this planet, and all that surrounds us, with new eyes as if you were looking at everything for the first time. This is when we need to be iconoclasts. Do not assume anything; just observe with an open mind. Soon you will see that what you thought were major differences between human and non-human beings are indeed similarities dressed in different clothes. They are more detectable in those we call animals but extend to all living species, although they are not easily identifiable because let's keep in mind that our eyes are human and, therefore, limited by human mindset and comprehension, even when prejudice has been restrained.

So far, all that evolution has done for the human species seems to be limited to practical physical and mental abilities but no spiritual development has yet fully arisen from them. It is interpreted that Darwin thought, or wished, that at a certain point of equilibrium in human evolution, the species might evolve through cooperation and solidarity, compassion and extended awareness rather than physically. Sadly, to this day, such a trend has not manifested itself, notwithstanding the fact that some movements, such as the hippies in the Sixties, the

Greens and others, have timidly attempted a paradigm shift; but they were soon neutralised and engulfed by the rampant greedy materialism nourished by an ever-growing ruthless capitalism of the worst kind. 'Moral Darwinism' must wait!

11

THE OTHER WAY

Ethics and other concepts

A beautiful sentence that I cherish was uttered by my Rio do Tempo communicators years ago. One day, unexpectedly, they told me "There is another world; there is another way" and I was thrilled because considering that my communicators have never told me a lie, to know that there is another world with "very different values from ours" is a joy.

We live in a world that we, humans, have corrupted and degenerated to the ultimate level. Or perhaps, it is possible to go even lower? Maybe, and this thought makes me cry and despair. What a curse to have to wait to transit into the next dimension to finally live in a fair world! But at least we have that hope and this is already a solace. Injustice and cruelty towards the innocent, the feeble, the helpless, whoever they are, cause me great anxiety and I have enormous difficulty in coping with the situation but this is how our world acts as a whole and, sadly, individually, too.

A world of Truth

I have spoken a lot about the truth in preceding chapters and I will continue because I deem the truth to be the most important, albeit the rarest of all values in our world. When I asked Rio do Tempo which was the highest principle in their world, the straightforward reply came in English uttered by an imposing masculine voice: "The Truth!" Was this key information conveyed by the Technician or by another higher being? I have no way of knowing for sure but I would suspect it was the former.

On another occasion, I enquired about the meaning of the anomalous image of a mask that our little ITC group had received on my computer screen, and they explained "A máscara é a maneira de te dizer que o nosso mundo descobre a verdade" (The mask is our way of telling you that our world reveals the truth). This enigmatic statement could be interpreted in the sense that their world comes closer to the truth than our world, which is built on appearances and pretence (thus, the metaphor of the mask). Consequently, their world unveils the real nature of everyone and everything.

From a more prosaic point of view, it could mean that in the next dimension we will not be able to lie or to pretend. Lies have no place in their new life. It has been repeated over and over again that the beings of the next world perceive each other's thoughts as they perceive our own thoughts. "We know all your thoughts", they told several ITC operators, myself included. It is not uncommon to receive a reply to a question, which had not been properly formed in our mind before it is spoken. I give an example of a remarkable incident of this kind in my book *Electronic Voices, Contact with Another Dimension?* (Cardoso, 2010).

At the request of Professor David Fontana, I once put the following question to Rio do Tempo: "Is your world a world of thought?" I mentioned this episode in one of my previous books, as well as Rio do Tempo's unexpected response: "Our world is closer to the truth than your world [ours]" (see Cardoso ibid,

2010). However, to which truth does this statement allude? Is it ultimate reality? Is it closer to the source and to a profound awareness? Perhaps. Or was it a response to David Fontana's implied assumption that the next world is less real than our world because it is a world of thought (constructed through thinking) and not a world of matter? Did they mean that thought is real and [our] matter is illusory thus, is their world closer to reality than ours? I believe they might mean that but we cannot be sure. There seem to be a thousand paths to arrive at a possible understanding of the metaphors.

The deceased Raudive stressed in Luxembourg that in the next world he lived in accordance with his true being. He avowed that in our world he had lived under a false image of himself, pretending to be what was not his true nature. I translate his words:

> On the third plane of the Beyond, man meets his true self. When I lived on your side, I tried to be another person, different from the one I really was. The majority of people try to show an image of themselves, which is not the one that truly reflects them. Presently, being here, I recognise more my true self (Schäfer, 1992, p. 104).

The third plane of the Beyond is the level from where our Rio do Tempo communicators speak.

Which considerations can we surmise from the statements above? In my opinion they indicate progression. Their world "is closer to the Truth", closer to ultimate reality, than our world. We know that progression, evolution, is a fundamental goal of life on this planet. We know this is true in terms of our physical world and maybe it is true for all unknown worlds and for the likely infinite cosmos. The law of evolution regulates the many physical forms of life that inhabit the Earth. But 'to be closer to the Truth' implies a non-physical state, a transcendental or spiritual level, if we wish to call it that. Therefore, the rule of evolution applies to other levels of the being and of existence, not only to the physical level.

They call their world "a pure world", and one of the reasons for that is surely because "it is closer to the Truth". In a memorable DRV transmission, a powerful and clear masculine voice repeated several times "Our world is a pure world" and "your world [ours] is not good for us". An excerpt from this long communication from Rio do Tempo is in Example 21 MUNDO PURO of my CD 'Electronic Voices'. There are other very interesting affirmations in this audio but I am only quoting those with regard to the purity of the next world.[10] Nevertheless, I believe that our dear communicators do not possess the Truth, either. They are also searching for it.

The equality of all life

We know that within the cosmic order, the highest order, all beings in this world (and most probably in other worlds of which we cannot speak because we know nothing about them) are not only worth the same but obey the same laws; on our planet the visible differences are the result of different mental structures and physical shapes. Therefore, the little ant or mosquito that we kill involuntarily (or voluntarily), may also have a predetermined time of death because our ITC communicators speak from a universal perspective. We will discuss this issue in the next chapter.

The equality of all life is clearly one of the main features in the next world. In one of Hildegard Schäfer's ITC books, we find the transcription of a telephone conversation of June 2, 1988 between Swejen Salter from Timestream Station and Maggy Harsch-Fischbach, the Luxembourg ITC operator. Swejen told Maggy:

> ... Around 3,700 seals on the coast of Schleswig-Holstein, are threatened of (with) extinction. They suffer from herpes, which causes a kind of pneumonia. The

---

[10] http://www.itcjournal.org/?product=electronic-voices-cd-in-mp3-format

main reason is the pollution of the sea. We are trying to help from here. Do not forget that in the perspective of our world, animals' lives must be protected, also. In case people in your land think that we are worrying too much about the animals, it would be good if they understood that, in our sphere, one life has the same value as the other one ... (Schäfer, H. 1992, p. 202). Nothing could be more explicit

In my book *Electronic Voices, Contact with Another Dimension?* I cited the example of the DRV that replied to my question about the [spiritual] growth of non-human animals in the next world by saying: "They also try to know more". Moreover, a masculine voice that identified as Homero's, declared at my house via a DRV: "Homero, Homero, Homero! This is Rio de todo. This is Rio de todos. This is Rio do Tempo!" (Homer, Homer, Homer! This is the river of the whole. This is the river of all. This is Rio do Tempo!). Both affirmations perfectly match Swejen's information about the equal value of all life in the next world.

Let me clarify that in my opinion names like Homer, as the one used by this communicator, does not mean that we are listening to the great Greek poet, Homer. And, on another occasion, a communicator from Rio do Tempo Station announced himself as Platão (Plato) and here, again, I believe this to be just an eccentricity. Maybe some communicators much admire the great classical figures and therefore, like to use their names for themselves. Or maybe their real names in this world were indeed Homero or Platão, although I have never met anyone so called. Or maybe there is something else that we cannot figure out. Naturally, what I deem less likely is that we are actually listening to the great classical figures. Although in an unexplained field like our discipline nothing is impossible. Prospective ITC operators should keep my remarks in mind when confronted with these fairly common situations in order to avoid subjecting our field of research to more mockery and abuse.

Hierarchies

Some people seem to be taken aback when I say that hierarchies also exist in the next dimension of life, but this is what different ITC operators have been told, myself included. Higher beings of non-human nature, part of a hierarchy, as they themselves avowed, manifested repeatedly, e.g. to the Harsch-Fischbachs in Luxembourg, at Rivenich with Adolf Homes, in Darmstadt with Peter Härting and his group and perhaps during other less well-known ITC experiments.

Indeed, different groups and stations in the Beyond have confirmed the existence of superior powers. I received the information from my Rio do Tempo partners but when I asked them if the hierarchies in their world were based on the same principles we follow in our world – regrettably, power, money, social status and so on – they replied that they were completely different. Obviously this information falls within the framework of the next world's set of values, so very different from ours as we have discussed above: "A similar world [in physical terms], albeit much more beautiful and with totally different values" to condense in a few words what the communicators have told ITC operators all over the world.

The interpretation of the concepts

Unfortunately, the mystery that surrounds many concepts put across by our communicators have not been resolved at this time.

The difficulties are colossal, as I have tried to pinpoint throughout this book. And they are of different etiology – technical, psychological, social, cultural to cite the predominant.

Let me recap what the famous high entity known as the Technician informed us 25 years ago:

> What you receive from our reality are mostly distorted radio signals, which for this reason are frequently

misinterpreted. It is up to the science of tomorrow to develop receiving devices; above all codes for translation into your language, like the set theory and the symbolic logic in mathematics has done already. It is very important and right that antennas of hundreds of meters diameter are built on traces of the radio signals from the universe. It might perhaps be still more important that minimum-size devices be invented in which 5-dimensional field impulses could be registered, possibly directly and not only via the detour over the nerves of the animals, of men or of rabbits. We could draw some hope from the fact that the human brain in regard to receiving techniques appears to have the first possibilities. This could be pioneering.
(Senkowski, 1995, ibid).

The Technician warned, as well, that "the majority of people are not yet ready [to understand] this kind of relationship between dimensions. They make mistakes about the content of the messages and do not understand what they mean. A great number of people try to obtain from us what they cannot get on the earth" (Locher and Harsch, 1995, p. 163-164).

I am very keen to draw my readers' attention to this situation so that they realise there is always a margin for error in what we, ITC operators – albeit mostly in good faith – postulate as coming from the next world. Naturally, the case is particularly pertinent when we offer information received telepathically.

12

THE BEWILDERING MEANING
OF FREE WILL

Does free will really exist?

The communicators have conveyed to us different statements, apparently contradictory, about the doubtful concept of free will, much extolled in the Western world but not so well regarded in other latitudes.

The Technician asserted: "Not a grain of sand will follow its path without it being foreseen in the universal plan".

In Darmstadt, the high entity ABX Juno, also of non-human nature, told Peter Härting and Jochem Fornoff the following: "Take good note of one thing. Free will is the outcome of the human capacity that renders man capable of understanding the good in its pure and whole state." On December 2nd 1987, the same ABX Juno sent a special message to Peter Härting "Tell Mr. Härting: just as you are free to act, you are free to refuse to act. Where you can say no, you can also say yes." (Schäfer, 1992, French Ed., p. 186 & p. 190- 191).

Are these statements contradictory? Perhaps not, but to our human mentality, they certainly seem paradoxical. Paradox is one of the main features of the communications from the next level of existence. In my opinion a major error we make when analysing the latter is to evaluate the information that our communicators send us, from our earthly, extremely limited perspective.

My readers will recall the Technician's recommendation of over 30 years ago, stating that people in general are not prepared to comprehend the information that our communicators convey to us and, consequently, ITC would be denigrated. How right the Technician was! ITC has already been denigrated and not only on account of the anti-paradigmatic content of the messages. Regrettably, many operators are to blame because the lack of respect that afflicts our discipline is chiefly caused by a number of them publicly distributing supposed anomalous voices or images which are nothing of the sort. They are simply optical or auditory delusions incorrectly interpreted and labeled, which a normal person cannot take seriously.

Anyhow, going back to our discussion, are we ruled by destiny, by ourselves or by unknown, hypothetical, "higher beings"? The subject has always puzzled me. Is free will real or merely illusory? If it is real, is it limited or absolute? Regrettably, so far, I have never asked Rio do Tempo about free will but I asked about other things of the same ilk. For instance, I enquired if chance existed. To this my communicators replied "Há o acaso, sim!" (Chance exists, yes!).

Conversely, Rio do Tempo asserted that death is the predetermined fate for all beings as I reported in a previous book. The same information was transmitted to other ITC operators as well.

I know there are Spiritualists and mediums who maintain we choose the time of death. When my first book *Electronic Voices* came out, one of my critics was Professor Imants Barušs. He published in the *Journal of Scientific Exploration*, Vol. 25, No 3, the following:

Review of *Electronic Voices: Contact with Another Dimension?*

Last Fall, a medium whom I had invited to give a guest lecture in one of my classes, had a message for one of the students from the student's great-grandmother who had lived into her 90s before dying of old age: "You choose the time of your death", [she said]. So who is right? Cardoso's "communicators" or my student's "great-grandmother"? During an ITC experiment that I conducted in my laboratory, the same medium had the impression that the level from which electronic apparatuses could be affected was analogous to a rough neighbourhood in which one could get mugged (Barušs, 2007). Decent people do not go there. That leaves the pretenders, liars, stray thought forms, astral goons, et al., and the occasional brave relative who has no idea how to affect the radios, tape recorder, or whatever. There is no reason to suppose, even if we have made contact with someone or something at some other level of reality, that they know what they are talking about, even if they pretend that they do.

Naturally, I could not agree less and I will go over my reasons. Prof. Barušs compares a medium's message with one of my Direct Radio Voice messages about the time of death, and firmly argues that it has more weight than the objective information (it can be heard by anybody), which I received from communicators who say they are sending us information from a station in the next world. Prof. Barušs does not question the accuracy of the medium's previous work, does not give any details of his/her communications and its accuracy, as is the usual procedure. To tell the truth, the whole account seems misleading to me.

    1. To start with, a medium's message is received subjectively and it is often difficult to verify its accuracy except in very exceptional cases duly referenced in the literature.

2. It is well known that many mediums – fortunately not all – are antagonistic towards ITC and EVP. Their reasons are a mystery to me but I suppose they could be related to the fear of losing clients and the income they derive from them; in short, prestige and power. Otherwise, how could we understand the dismissive, I would say offensive, harangue against all in the next dimension who communicate via EVP or ITC? – "… the level from which electronic apparatuses could be affected was analogous to a rough neighbourhood in which one could get mugged … "

3. I will not deny that there are accounts of pernicious EVP messages but in the majority of such cases, perhaps in all of them, those incidents are related to the low level of the EVP operator on the Earth, either from an ethical perspective or from his or her inner uncontrolled, exaggerated fears.

4. In addition, to my knowledge, there are no harmful communications, which originate from a station, or transmitting centre, in the next world. The most advanced contacts such as the DRV, the anomalous computer images, the telephone calls and computer texts need a station and the permission of a "higher being" to be conveyed to our dimension. This point has been highlighted by communicators of the highest wisdom and ethics – some of non-human origin – to Friedrich Jürgenson, Dr. Konstantin Raudive, the Harsch-Fischbach couple in Luxembourg, Adolf Homes in Germany and myself from Rio do Tempo Station, to cite the ones I am familiar with.

I said in my previous book that the voice, which affirmed on the time of death, was a DRV, and Prof. Baruš must know the difference between an EVP voice and a DRV (Direct Radio Voice). I will repeat the content of the loud, clear voice – consecutive statements in answer to my question about the time of death: 'Time of death is predetermined for each being'; 'it is predetermined, yes'; 'it is predetermined, you may take the step and [make] the commitment'; 'of course it is predetermined' (literal translation from the original in Portuguese). There are some five affirmative answers to my question, one following the other, in that recording. Hans Otto König's communicators used practically the same words: 'The time of death is predetermined for each life' (Schäfer, 1993, Portuguese ed. p.100).

The existence of stations has been fully documented

The existence of stations in the next dimension has been documented even before EVP/ITC first occurred in our world. As an example, I will cite the renowned English writer and journalist William T. Stead, who purportedly communicated with his daughter Estelle via a medium (and writer) of exceptional reputation, Pardoe Woodman. In chapter VII of *The Blue Island: Experiences of a New Arrival Beyond the Veil*, Stead (who had died in the Titanic disaster) speaks of "a house", "a building given over to this kind of work", i.e. communication with the earth (Stead, 1922).

My group of communicators from Rio do Tempo station speak of the "hemicycle of Tempo" from where they transmit. Carlos de Almeida in one of his dialogues with me, finished the evening's contact with these words: ... "Ele não vem e ao meu grupo desço" (He does not come and I go down to my group), and continued: "Vou à Alma!" (I go to the Soul!); when I called "Rio do Tempo!", the anomalous voice almost shouted: "É o edifício do Tempo (It is the building of Tempo [Rio do Tempo]), é o hemiciclo do Tempo (It is the hemicycle of Tempo). See example 6 of the DRV, Vou à Alma, in the CD 'Electronic Voices'.[11]

In Luxembourg, the Technician and Swejen Salter from Zeitstrom (Timestream) station were able to send an anomalous computer image of the transmission building and called it "The Tower". And in conversations with Maggy Harsch and the participants at their reunions, they also spoke of the station's hemicycle – curved or semicircular structure (Locher and Harsch, 1992 ibid).

Furthermore, some of the DRV messages that I received at the beginning of my Rio do Tempo contacts start by "Torre,

---

[11] http://www.itcjournal.org/?p=4621

torre, é o Rio do Tempo!" (Tower, tower, it's Rio do Tempo!). The masculine voice was so loud that it could be heard in my very large garden while my studio is on the second floor of the house, and when I digitised it I cut the line entry volume by 40 per cent, otherwise the sound peak would be too loud and deafening. The same utterances were repeated on several occasions during that month of October 1998.[12] More than similarities, I believe we can consider these perfect matches.

But William Stead had already described some of his after death experiences through another medium. Under the heading "A Great Republic", in a Harbinger of Light article dated June 1st 1912, Stead explains what he found in the spirit world. The description is long but I will highlight what interests us for the purposes of our discussion:

> … There it was explained to me that conditions have to be made for perfect communication that machinery, so to speak, for sending messages through the ether had to be studied. Here, also, are schools of learning for those who needed instruction even in the rudiments of spiritual knowledge; here were vast enterprises that included work in glorious regions of which those in earth life and in the fog of material selfish thought can form no idea … "

Many other descriptions similar to what we learn nowadays from our communicators' messages can be found in Stead's post-mortem writings. I believe that situations described over 100 years ago, such as those I mentioned above (there are many others), are of extreme importance for our study and understanding of what is happening in the field of electronic communication with the deceased. They imply the existence of a common pattern in the next dimension of life as I put forward and thoroughly illustrated in my book *Electronic Contact with the Dead, What Do the Voices Tell Us?* (Cardoso, 2017).

---

[12] An example can be found at: http://www.itcjournal.org/?p=4690

Going back to my opinion of Prof. Barušs' review, I would recommend that before insulting such a valuable means of contact and communication between this and the next world, the pertinent literature is read and studied. Not only the titles in the English language, of course, but all of it. There are over 100 titles in ITC literature alone. Furthermore, I submit that the failure to replicate the EVP phenomenon published by Prof. Barušs in the *Journal of Scientific Exploration*, Vol. 15, No. 3, pp. 355–367, 2001, should not be a measure of the validity of the phenomenon. As the communicators have stated and the author recognises in his article, "Spirituality is a determinant factor to achieve ITC contacts". There must be many other reasons as also stated by the communicators. Thus, and since unfortunately they cannot all be assessed because we ignore them, we need to be humble and be aware of the fact that we know so very little. Moreover, perhaps we are not yet ready to understand and accept such challenging information.

I could go on discussing the JSE 2001 article by Prof. Barušs; for example, the possibility that the disparity in the interpretation of the anomalous electronic voices by different people is due to the varied 'phonemic [perceptual] restoration' effect produced by the different linguistic archives of their brains.[13] And, once more, I insist that we know so very little! It is certainly better not to jump to conclusions at this stage, particularly before insulting a whole field of research, its operators and its initiators – the purported communicators from another dimension.

I would finish by suggesting to Prof Barušs that he uses the same level of rigour rightly applied to his EVP experiments, with the messages received by his medium who affirmed that "we choose the time of our death". No controls of whatever kind are mentioned in his report.

Nevertheless, many other reputable mediums say exactly the opposite of Prof Barušs' medium. Once more, I recall one of the

---

[13] https://www.researchgate.net/publication/257291312_Perceptual_Restoration_of_Missing_Speech_Sounds).

greatest – Marcel Belline, the "Prince of the Clairvoyants" as he was called. In the famous dialogues with his deceased son Michel, Belline asked the young man if it was a mechanical malfunctioning of his car or another reason that had been the cause of his fatal accident. The boy replied: "No, my hour had come. I had to leave." (Belline, 1972, p 110).

It was Tico-Tico's time!

Still pondering the question of the time of death, recently I remembered an incident from many years ago, perhaps in 1998. Unwittingly, Tico-Tico, the two-year old puppy I had adopted, was the subject of an occurrence related to the time of death. It was a sunny day in May and I had returned happily, with a number of my former abandoned dogs and my Doberman puppy Lady, from a walk in the forest around my house in Vigo, Spain, where I lived.

I had an invitation that Sunday for lunch at the home of friends and I proceeded to take a shower and get dressed to go to their house nearby. I said good-bye to all the dogs (some five or six at the time) and, not being able to find Tico-Tico, searched for him all around the garden, calling him loudly. I finally found him asleep under the shade of a tree and went to pet him and say good-bye to him. To my great surprise he did not react and I persisted in trying to wake him up. I never did because he was dead. I couldn't believe it because Tico-Tico was a happy, healthy, lively little dog with no known ailment whatsoever. I was truly stunned.

The next time I experimented with the DRV (I was already receiving them frequently) I asked my communicators what had happened to Tico-Tico. Their loud, adamant reply, which I recorded, asserted: "It was his time!"

If we believe, as I do, what our communicators tell us about the time of death, other difficult questions arise. Such as, for example, what is the role of a healthy lifestyle in longevity? Is this also programmed? Because we must accept the proven fact that longevity has increased in the last centuries due to health care, new medication and healthier and more relaxed lifestyles. If the time of death is predetermined, how do we explain these factors? Is it all part of a grand divine plan that gives us the impression that we command something but in reality we do not? This is the most plausible response – at least to my eyes – but one, which, once again, cannot be proven (or disproven).

Recently, I watched an interesting documentary on the concept of guilt in neuroscience. The neuroscientist, a Professor from Harvard University, whose name I cannot recall, indicated that the brain was 'programmed' to execute certain acts, for instance to commit a violent crime, as a result of chromosome configuration.

I believe this is not to say that everything is already programmed in the configuration of the brain. We just don't know. But what is and what isn't? As we saw in a previous chapter, Adolf Homes' communicators informed us about "the programmed consciousness": ".... With the physical end of the individual the programmed consciousness changes...", but not of its extent. Is it all programmed? Of course we do not know the answer to that.

Thus, what are we? Each being living a cosmic experience? No good, no bad, just experience? God, or the Principle, 'learning', 'expanding', through the experiences of each one of us – humans, non-humans, plants, minerals? I suppose it is possible.[14]

---

[14] Readers will have noticed that God is called "The Principle" throughout this book. Indeed, the high entities that mentioned God at Maggy and Jules Harsch-Fischbach's and at Adolf Homes' studios averred: "God or the Principle".

We should remember that they spoke in German and the exact words were: "Das Prinzipium von Allem-was-ist. GOTT IST DAS PRINZIP selbst". That is, the origin of all things, not a being, not an entity, not the principal, but The Origin.

13

THE GREAT ITC ACHIEVEMENT

Where does all this take us?

After many years of reflection, I reached the conclusion that the most important feature of our marvelous contacts with another dimension is the change in mentality, which they are bound to bring about. Naturally, this does not mean that communication with our deceased loved ones is not important in its own right. Conversely, it is a magnificent proof of what I would call the divine glory. I quote Darwin to clarify my position:

> I cannot pretend to throw the least light on such abstruse problems [the existence of God]. The mystery of the beginning of all things is insoluble to us; and I for one must be content to remain an Agnostic.

> But Darwin also stated in his autobiography: ... [A] source of conviction in the existence of God ... follows from the extreme difficulty or rather impossibility of conceiving this immense and wonderful universe, including man with his capability of looking far

backwards and far into futurity, as the result of blind chance or necessity. When thus reflecting … I deserve to be called a Theist (Darwin, 1958).

I also associate myself with him in that reflection.

Our fantastic communications are certainly a gift of nature, of God, if we prefer to describe "All-That-Is" in that way. And we are certainly privileged to participate in this interdimensional bridge, even if we do it through much work, dedication and perseverance.

I believe our dear partners, those who preceded us on the road, are right when they tell us what a beautiful masculine voice chanted years ago at my studio via the DRV: "Nós somos vós, somos todos pobres homens!" (We are you; we are all poor men!). (See CD Electronic Voices, Chant 2). I also believe that they do not know God any more than we do.

The positive side of seeing life and the world in a different way through our partners' contacts has, nonetheless, depressing consequences, if I may so call them, as I have amply described above. We feel outcasts in a standard society of common thinking; therefore we feel lonelier. We can no longer look at life the way others do. But this feeling of marginalisation somehow makes us feel closer to our communicators. The awareness of belonging to our unknown and invisible Group-Soul truly develops (On the Group-Soul see Cardoso, 2010, 2017).

The contacts with our deceased loved ones have improved the lives of many people

As I mentioned above, at Marcello Bacci's Centre in Grosseto, hundreds of parents re-established their lives, regained hope and joie de vivre through the DRV that allowed them to communicate with their deceased children and other loved ones. I spoke with several of these parents during my visits to Grosseto and they unanimously confirmed their conviction that, to their great satisfaction, they had been in contact with their children and loved family members.

Similarly, my dear friend, the French pioneer Monique Simonet, put hundreds of people in contact with their deceased loved ones to their great relief and joy, this time through EVP voices. Monique Simonet was a wonderful person and a great transcommunicator (See Simonet, 1991, 1993, 2001). She was also the founder of the French Association 'Infinitude', later directed by Monique and Jacques Blanc-Garin who continued her work.

In the USA the Association TransCommunication did similar work with its many members. The German Association for Transcommunication Research (VTF) has also developed very positive work in our field. There will be other associations and institutions all over the world but I am less familiar with them and so I apologise for not mentioning them individually.

Years ago I paid Monique Simonet a visit at her house, in Reims, and asked her permission to record our conversation. She gladly agreed and we talked for a long time. We had a very enjoyable occasion, the memory of which I cherish. My friend Carlos Fernández accompanied me on that trip and he videoed the conversation. I must confess that, so far, given the many and frequent interruptions I have had to make in my ITC work, I did not watch the video but, upon my return, I listened thoroughly to the audio recordings and what a wonderful surprise I had! The talk between Monique and me was full of merry comments by voices other than our own, definitely not produced in the house where only the three of us and Monique's lovely cat were present. The many comments I recorded were totally pertinent to our conversation and the anomalous voices were as loud and clear as our own voices: a memorable occasion, indeed.

The many people who, throughout the years, have come to me to ask for direction or help with their distraught lives have also stated that ITC changed their lives in a very positive way. I am sure this feeling is common to all ITC operators because we are all approached by people who need support and help, particularly when they endure grief. From my side I prefer to show people how to try the contacts for themselves and I have done it on a great number of occasions. Most of the people who came to me and asked for guidance in their own EVP experiments reported positive results and this has given me great satisfaction.

An extraordinary ITC occurrence

One of those was Guillermo Campos from Seville who came to visit me last year. I reported the whole story in a paper published in my Blog under the title: "Report on an extraordinary ITC occurrence: A visit with unsuspected results".[15]

At least for some months, the electronic voices that he received continued addressing me, often pronouncing my name, my father's and my brother's names, Só's and even my dog Surya's name. This happened at his house as if the communicators did not know that it was Guillermo listening and not me directly. These DRVs seem to be exact replicas, in all aspects, of Rio do Tempo's DRV that manifested at my house throughout many years. They are invariably in Portuguese and repeat the same sentences. Moreover, they sometimes say "trabalho" (work) in the middle of the long voice sequences as they used to do at my house. On one of these occasions a masculine voice uttered: "O Rio é mais grande do que parece!" (The river is larger than it seems). Maybe this was a good explanation of the situation, i.e. the river comprises my house, Guillermo's house and who knows how many more. I think this could be a good reading of the metaphor.

Recently, during the pandemic quarantine, one of Rio do Tempo's DRVs repeated at Guillermo's house, "O ódio já está em casa" (Hatred is already at home) and "O ódio atacou cá em casa!" (Hatred attacked here at home!). My interpretation is that they were referring to Covid-19. But I have no way of knowing for sure. I have lost contact with Guillermo, so I don't know if he continues to receive Rio do Tempo's DRV. But I know that because the voices spoke in Portuguese, a language that he did not know at all, it was somehow discouraging for him.

---

[15] https://itcanabelacardoso.wordpress.com

During the same experiment on March 30, 2020, my father spoke and identified himself clearly, "I am the father, João Cardoso" (translation) repeating the sentences several times. My brother Luis also spoke on a couple of occasions and gave his full name, while my dog Só identified himself, too. Só articulated clearly and loudly "Fala o Só" (It is Só speaking) several times. Interestingly, at the beginning of the DRV session, a masculine voice uttered "Nós estamos bem" (We are well).

The Expansion of Human Consciousness

We know about some attributes of the next world from my own work as well as from that of other ITC operators. Among the former, as I have extensively quoted in previous books and papers, is the situation of living outside of time in another dimension, the equality of all life, the possibility of being in several places at the same time, the illusory condition of form or appearance, the power of thought and of telepathic communication between all beings, and the nonexistence of death, to quote the most relevant aspects. Using our limited and deficient human language, we would summarise these conditions as being more advanced. Thus, we could go step by step and learn from what our dear communicators tell us.

It is easy to conclude from what I have posited that the main goal of ITC is to contribute to the expansion of human consciousness, starting by the expansion of the operator's consciousness. The communicators have reiterated this purpose on numerous occasions. In Luxembourg, the Technician stated, "ITC is the most important instrument to make human consciousness get out of its state of sleepiness. To achieve this goal we need bridges and builders between your world and the world of the spirit ... " (Schäfer 1993, pp. 113-114).

It is also reported that the deceased Konstantin Raudive spoke about the importance of the expansion of human consciousness during a post-mortem telephone conversation with a French lady, Aline Piget, in 1997. During this remarkable event, the first one of its kind in France, Raudive affirmed: "I would like you to know, dear Aline, that the object of an earthly life is not just the goodness. The object is to be conscious ... " (Théry, P., 2000, *ITC Journal*, 2, pp 42-43).

Rio do Tempo put it in a simpler way, "We speak to the world, everywhere, the opening of the way!" (translation from the Portuguese original).

Naturally, the expansion of human consciousness would imply an important transformation – above all a change of paradigm. The latter would principally mean a change of our thought patterns. Naturally, a true change in our thinking models would mean the release of human prejudices, which prevent recognising the existence of the soul (the divine principle) of all beings, the equality of, and respect for, all life; it would lead to the social and financial organisation of the world under a different model that would not have money as the priority ... and so on, and so on. Overall, it would mean, perhaps, that our lives would be similar to those of our dear communicators, except that we, as mortals, would not enjoy their extraordinary capacities, which, as my communicators have stated, "pertain to their dimension".

This sounds very utopian, of course, but I am speaking of an expansion of consciousness. I doubt that such a transformation could be accomplished suddenly but perhaps we could go step by step and maybe this is what Raudive meant.

Again, in Luxembourg the Technician stated, "The respect for each living being belongs to the further spiritual development of man" and recommended that "In the future ITC should comprise human rights and the protection of animals and of Nature".

On another occasion, the high entity insisted, "The inhabitants of the Earth must learn to change their thought pattern ... some will recognise, through ITC, the worthlessness of their material inclinations and will turn to spiritual interests." And, addressing Maggy Harsch, communicated, "You have the task to divulge what I am telling you" (Locher and Harsch, 1992, Portuguese translation p. 126, 127).

We desperately need a paradigm shift to be brought about by the expansion of human consciousness but will we be able to carry it out? Utopia, perhaps, but little by little we should attempt to evolve and perhaps one day we will, at last, reach it. I like to quote my communicators when, from time to time, they say unexpectedly in the middle of a DRV contact: "Oremos!" (Let us pray!). Yes, dear readers, let us pray for the change to happen.

The electronic voices make us question the existence of God

In my previous book, *Electronic Contact with the Dead*, I discussed briefly the concept of God. What do we mean by God? There are those who personify God and I apologise for not discussing that perspective but despite its popularity with millions of followers, I do not think it bears much weight from a reasonable point of view. The Technician emphasised the human error regarding God: "Man makes up the idea of God according to his human representations and his own image. God or the Principle is not comparable to anything that exists." (see Locher and Harsch, ibid, 1995, p. 148). There is one very important affirmation in this statement: "God or the Principle". Therefore, God and the Principle are the same.

At Marcello Bacci's Centre in Grosseto, the communicators made this extraordinary remark, as usual through the DRV, "Nobody is as close to God as an atheist. You wouldn't be looking for mc if you hadn't found mc!" (Capitani and Pagnotta, 1990, p. 212).

Filipe, my beloved communicator from Rio do Tempo, uttered this remark during his long intervention, which I called Power of Infinity: " ... The unconscious of God covers all ... ". [16]

Next day I expressed my surprise at the statement and told Rio do Tempo: I thought God was absolute consciousness but

---

[16] http://www.itcjournal.org/?p=4621

Filipe spoke about the unconscious of God; a feminine voice replied immediately, even before I finished my sentence: "So did I! Only God knows!"

Do our beloved relatives and friends in the next dimension of life know God? I do not think so. In 2011, a low masculine voice replied to my recurrent question about God's existence with: "We don't know if it [God] exists". I presume that communicator was a deceased human, not a high entity of a different nature as was the case at the Harsch-Fischbach's or at Adolf Homes'.

I believe God is unknowable. Or maybe God is many. God is perhaps a multiple, dynamic process constantly changing and evolving from the life experiences of all of us – from the tiniest grain of sand to the humblest fly and most powerful human in the never-ending evolutionary journey of awareness of all life throughout the worlds.

One of Marcello Bacci's DRV communicators is reported to have said in Grosseto: "God is the silence proper" (Bacci, 1991). In one of my subjective interactions with Rio do Tempo, those I call telepathic impressions, I asked my communicators if God was the silence. Their reply was "God is everything that exists".

And one of the extraordinary messages received by Adolf Homes, purportedly from high entities, stated the following:

God consists of incomprehensible cosmic values and neither heaven nor hell has anything to do with It.

God is the principle proper, the cause of everything that exists. God is in every being.

God is in everything.

The concept of God is an information.

[But] your concept of God is an idea projected by yourselves.

In Professor Senkowski's compilation of Homes' messages, there are two pages devoted to God and the human concept of God. I have translated a few lines from the Italian translation (See Senkowski, 1999, Italian translation pp. 38-39; German original pp. 34,35). Basically, the high beings who communicated, mainly via computer texts, differentiate God, the real 'God of the Origins' that contains (is in) everything, from the gods created by man and the different religions, to which they do not attribute any value but, instead, truly harmful meaning and actions.

> The information of the divine of the origins has become foreign to you. The plan of the original creation was manipulated by pseudo-gods.

> Discord and ambition are a consequence of secondary gods ... (Senkowski ibid, Italian translation, p. 35).

Homes' communicators assert that the pseudo-gods constantly try, and achieve, the destruction of the God of the Origins, the primal God, in the hearts and the minds of men. The God of the Origins is the Principle, the creator of all life. They say:

> The spirit of the primal God creates souls and worlds in both psychic and physical structures. Every being in the universe possesses – in its entirety – soul. The goodness and the love of the Omnipotence make the light of the eternal union shine in the souls. The essence of the soul, as well as the omnipotence of God, surpasses every possibility of expression. (Senkowski ibid, Italian translation, p. 12).

Actually, the existence of God as one independent being is a relatively recent concept, proclaimed by the theist religions. Those we call primitive peoples did not know about (and therefore did not question) God's existence; they knew only the spirits with whom they could communicate (Bozzano, 1941). In the Introduction to his excellent work, *Popoli Primitivi e manifestazioni supernormali*, Bozzano cites Grant Allen, who stated in *The Evolution of the Idea of God* (p. 42):

> "Religion contains an element much older than religion proper, much more fundamental and persistent than any belief in God or in the Gods … . That element is the belief in the survival of the dead". From his side, Huxley writes: "There are primitive peoples without a God in the true sense of the word, but there are not any, at any time, without 'spirits'." (Huxley, 1870, p. 163).

In reality, the question: 'Does God exist?' is in my view an idle one because even if It existed, we could not find out about It in an intellectually satisfactory manner. Therefore, we, humans, would continue doubting and questioning.

Masanobu Fukuoka, an enlightened sage whom I had the privilege of meeting and being in contact with when I lived in Tokyo, put it simply: "Only search for God those who do not know It. Animals and children do not seek God" (see Fukuoka, 1987). I must add that in my opinion the Japanese sage is basically right because the human search for God, or 'The Ultimate Truth', is driven by the intellect, not by emotions nor feelings, which seem to be the vital elements not only in the evolutionary spiral but also in spiritual growth or, as our communicators put it, in the expansion of consciousness of every being. After all, it seems that the quest should be a matter of the heart not of the mind. And the outcome, if any, a magnificent victory of the heart!

14

CONDITIONS TO RECEIVE THE ELECTRONIC VOICES

What factors are involved in achieving ITC?

A t this point I am sure that many of my readers will be asking this question. Indeed, interested people frequently ask me what the conditions to obtain ITC contacts are. I have written a lot about it elsewhere but I will summarise here what I think is relevant and what the communicators have told us on this matter.

Firstly, I will start by the technical questions. In Luxembourg the Technician advised us:

> So that we may possibly achieve this type of contacts through radios, it will be necessary to cultivate intensely the regular reception of microphone messages. Otherwise, the different groups from our side will not be able to adjust to the human voice. (Schäfer, 1992, p. 110).

Thus, I would recommend anybody interested in achieving more advanced contacts such as the DRV, to practise with the

EVP experimentation without feeling discouraged or lacking confidence or enthusiasm even if the voices are not forthcoming. Perseverance and patience are key factors in this field.

Years ago I asked Rio do Tempo what was the most important condition for the contact with their world and the immediate reply was: "Contact!", apparently implying that to attempt the contact is the most important factor in this process. They also told me when I inquired about the conditions for the establishment of the contacts: "There are no conditions" and "There is no psychic process!", while I had thought that a very sophisticated psychic condition from the part of the operator on the earth was important. But, on another occasion, people from Rio do Tempo avowed: "Everything counts [for achieving the contacts]".

The Technician averred in Luxembourg, "A pure heart and mind are important premises of the contacts with our dimension" (Harsch and Locher 1995, pp. 148). This high non-human being recommended:

> Modesty and gratitude must absolutely be cultivated. Modest people are often enlightened and they evidence a certain spiritual elevation … they contribute to the flourishing of harmony in their environment. In the measure that a person overcomes his or her vices and imperfections, he or she may expect a proportionate spiritual reward. Each one is given that which he or she needs (Harsch and Locher 1995, pp. 174).

Based on her own experience, Maggy Harsch-Fischbach explained:

> We sometimes had the impression that they did not always know what conditions were important for a good transmission and what was unimportant. Their answer to our question was mostly, "Communication depends on so many things!" (Harsch and Locher 1995, ibid).

In addition to the above, I believe there are some factors, which will favourably benefit the contacts. As we all know, it is said, "Seek and you will find". This maxim applies to almost everything in life and, likewise, to ITC. But it is also necessary to recognise its limits. If, for instance, we search for native polar bears in the wilderness of Africa we will not find any except for an exceptional circumstance and so on. Furthermore, I am speaking of things of a subtle nature which do not obey our physical laws. They have laws but we ignore them and certainly they are not the same laws. Nevertheless, "Seek and you will find" applies well to ITC.

True interest from the heart is an essential requisite

The key feature to drive us into the quest until we find, is simple and easy to explain – interest, deep, unwavering interest on the part of the researcher. Exceptionally, because there are not many conditions when it comes to justifying ITC results that I commit myself to, I believe this point to be of great importance. In Luxembourg, the well-known entity from Zeitstrom (Timestream) Station, Dr Swejen Salter, averred through a computer message (one of many), which appeared on the screen of Maggy and Jules Harsch-Fischbach's computer on May 10, 1990, "If there is sufficient interest in us on your side, we are real and able to intervene in occurrences on your side." (Senkowski, ibid 1995).

But there are different kinds of interest. I speak of a profound interest of the heart that nothing can deter. Naturally, this unwavering interest will entail a resolute commitment to the work. It might mean, for instance, long and inconvenient hours of waiting and carrying the equipment with us, if we travel, so as not to miss the predetermined recording schedules. You may have to cancel social commitments for the same reason, and so on. At Grosseto, Bacci's communicators were more precise. They affirmed: "...You must work to have a reply from the deceased" (Capitani and Pagnotta, p. 131).

I am not sure if it was in Luxembourg at the Harsch-Fischbach's or in Germany at Adolf Homes', but I believe it was the latter who received the message: "It is the interest of the medium that makes the contact happen." (Senkowski, 1995, ibid). The term 'medium' could apply to the traditional mediums of the Spiritualist tradition or to ITC operators who, albeit in a different way, also intermediate in the electronic communications. In his book Professor Senkowski also explained that the communicators conceive their reality as 'tangible and material' as we conceive our physical world. They do not see themselves as 'transparent ghosts/spiritual beings' (Senkowski, 1995, ibid).

Again at Marcello Bacci's Centre in Grosseto, the communicators asserted: "We must not forget that the energies were created because there was someone who sought them and sought for a new world that is not the end, rather it is the beginning of a new heaven" (Pagnotta, 1992, p. 27).

Thus, dear reader, be assured that a deep interest from the heart (and/or the mind) will work miracles in the establishment of ITC. When we speak of unwavering interest, a reflection comes to my mind. We all know – I speak of ITC operators and other people interested, or involved, in the research – that in many cases there is a time when the contacts diminish or even stop all together. As I mentioned in a previous chapter, I received no communication for almost two years but I persevered and they returned. Can we assume that Rio do Tempo's voices returned to my studio because I persevered? I suppose it is legitimate to believe so, although we cannot be absolutely sure that this was the reason or the only reason. Maybe it was one reason among many. We don't know. I emphasize, once more, that certainties do not belong in this area. Only probabilities.

Other aspects that I deem important are:

Tranquility – my communicators have emphasized over and over again that an inner state of tranquility is a very important factor for their work. They have told me often, and later also telepathically, "We need you to be very tranquil". But I must admit that I am not, by nature, a serene person, although recently they have told me: "We are happy because you are much more tranquil". But that depends on the days, or times, on the circumstances of my personal life. It is not a permanent state of mind. At Bacci's, the communicators avowed: "It is necessary to be in the disposition to discover serious things with utmost serenity".

Persistence and patience. In addition to what Friedrich Jürgenson pointed out to George Meek, as described above, at Bacci's Centre, the communicators affirmed, "We try the most possible to insert ourselves. Patience is required." And Bacci remarked about this statement, "Indeed psychophony is chiefly perseverance and patience" (Bacci, 1991, p. 82).

Open-mindedness. To accept the possibility that the deceased can speak with us through a radio or similar device needs a free, open mind. And, since the communication happens between two partners – the next world communicator and the Earth operator – it is possible that if the mind is closed, the message may not be able to come through, although it is technically mediated. The complex ways of this research and work do not allow us to make definitive statements but I believe this may be a reason.

Resonance, as the emotional affinity between the two partners of different dimensions is sometimes described in a symbolic way is, in my opinion, the golden key to strengthening ITC contacts. This intimate bond, the overpowering sensation of belonging to the group that communicates with us, develops as a result of the contacts. It is like finding an unknown part of ourselves, which, however, we recognise immediately as ours. I have recorded several affirmations from my ITC partners, which state, "És do Tempo" (You are from [Rio do] Tempo) or to each other, "Ela pertence ao Tempo" (She belongs to [Rio do] Tempo). In a way it is like finding a deep, intrinsic family that cannot be denied or questioned because it is part of you: a family that you cannot see but clearly feel – it embraces everything – the flowers and plants you love, the animals you cared for in an active or passive way, the rocks in your garden or elsewhere, the people you met and liked, the ones you admired, the ones you love or loved, perhaps even the material things that made your life more interesting and so on; maybe other beings, also, albeit not necessarily humans who share your interests and preferences, in short, who have a link with you, even though an unidentified one.

From **empathy, love** will naturally arise or maybe it is love that creates empathy. Yes, I think this is the way. The experimenter's love for his or her communicators: that special group, which you feel but do not see, can manifest in different ways and one of them is certainly through unremitting work. I found the following statement in Professor Senkowski's compilation of the extraordinary computer texts received by Adolf Homes: "Identification with us through compliance with the Natural Law: research, knowledge, patience, humility and love." (Senkowski, 1999, German original p. 34, Italian p. 68.).

The permission to contact us is the major prerequisite

In this book and in other works, I have discussed what appears to be the indispensable condition for our communicators to be able to contact our world – permission to do it (See Cardoso, 2017). Permission could be related to the passage and perhaps it applies to the most advanced contacts only, in our case the DRV. I am inclined to think so. Anyhow, they definitely need permission to contact us through ITC.

I do not know about the extent of this condition in other ways of communication, namely through mediums, but I have seen it mentioned in some mediumship reports, also, although I cannot recall the actual references. They need permission, as well, to inform us about, or even mention, certain issues.

Some time ago, I read a report by a French lady who claims to have received several telephone calls from her deceased son Yvan (Moreau, 2012). In a couple of those calls, there was a clear admonition about making the contact. One of them was even cut short by a very authoritarian voice that warned: "Message alerte, on n' a pas le droit" (message on the alert, one has not the right) and, on another occasion, "C'est dangereux par téléphone" (It's dangerous via telephone). I translate below an extract of the report published by Mme. Laurence Moreau in Le Messager (2012), 78, pp.14-15, under the title '6 « coups de fil » de l'au-delà' (Six telephone calls from the Beyond).

> I am at home, just returned from my office's Christmas party. The telephone rings. I pick up the 'phone but do not reply because I see that it is a hidden call. But I understand the following message clearly: "I call to give you a kiss" in, undoubtedly, Yvan's voice. Totally taken aback I record the message. At my computer I isolate something else: "It's me" (Yvan's timbre) and next "My little Laurence". This voice is more feminine; could it be my mother's? And then at the end "Message on the alert, one does not have the right!" in a very authoritarian tone and next it cuts sharp (our son is truly very disobedient in the beyond!) …

I have spoken about "permission" repeatedly; also because my communicators explicitly pointed out, in several instances, that authorisation was necessary for the establishment of the DRV contacts (see Cardoso, 2017).

Mme. Laurence Moreau reported that she could hear a babble of different voices speaking very rapidly in what formed a kind of acoustic background mingled with the words attributed to her deceased son. In many of Rio do Tempo's DRVs, in particular during the first years, the babble of voices in the background of a direct conversation between a specific communicator and me was also very noticeable. A number of those could be understood as a conversation going on among different people, sometimes about the talk under way with me while with others the content of the babble could not be deciphered. It was just a jabber of mixed voices not sufficiently loud and detached from each other to be understood correctly (Cardoso, 2010).

The Brazilian researcher previously cited, Oscar D' Argonnel, must have been the first one to report on this experience, but the same situation has been cited by other ITC operators starting with Friedrich Jürgenson (e.g. Alvisi 1976, 1983) and even by some mediums.

It is of great importance to research the literature and identify similar situations related to the communications common to operators who, overall, had no contact with each other or even knew of each other's work, as happened with the French lady. I suspect she had not read ITC literature, including my books and articles, but she noticed the most striking features of the occurrence without previously knowing about them. She even remarked: "Je ne comprends pas pourquoi on me dit : *C'est dangereux par téléphone* ...»" (I don't understand why I am told "*It's dangerous via the telephone*").

I think it is worthy of note to tell my readers how the question of the permission seems to cause great perplexity in people not acquainted with the phenomenon. I am frequently asked if such or such person with whom I had a special relationship, has made contact through ITC and when I reply that it did not happen, invariably my interlocutor seems to be really surprised. Sometimes he or she continues and asks, "And don't you find that strange?" At this point I speak about the indispensable permission to contact our world but I always get the impression that the concept is not properly understood and, even less, accepted. Nevertheless, believe me dear reader, this is absolutely correct. There are very strict laws in the next dimension and they are always obeyed. I am sure there is a mechanism to implement them and also that in the lack of fulfilment from our dear communicators' side, one of the consequences will be to be prevented from speaking again with his or her dear ones still on this plane.

I once asked Rio do Tempo if the permission to speak with us was difficult to obtain. Their clear reply was, "It is not difficult" but "to speak [with you] is difficult".

Still on another occasion, astonishingly, when I asked what was necessary to achieve the contact and be able to speak, the voices replied, "We don't know". Perhaps this is the reason why a voice utters triumphantly in almost all of the many DRVs I have received in the last years, "The voice has already passed!" or "The voice passed!" always in an exultant tone as I have posted in a previous chapter.

From my observation of my communicators' thousands of hours of work, I believe that intention, persistence, training, "great effort" and "love", as they themselves have asserted, are indispensable factors from their side for the success of ITC contacts. Actually, very similar conditions apply to our work here on the earth. Therefore, while bearing in mind the obvious differences between the two levels of existence, the multiple efforts, which they must make in order to speak with us, must match those on our side of life. From the very beginning, I tried to enquire of my communicators how I could help in their endeavours. Their first reply clearly said (literal translation), "You may help the communication, it means your work" as I told my readers in chapter 7. Very recently, I asked a similar question and they replied simply "Trabalho!" (Work!).

APPENDIX:
A HANDBOOK OF EVP:

WHAT YOU NEED TO KNOW TO ATTEMPT THIS METHOD OF ELECTRONIC CONTACT WITH THE DEAD

Dear Reader:

Here you will find an EVP Manual, which contains the practical points that I deem relevant for EVP work. Please remember that all ITC experiments should start with EVP work, as recommended by our partners from another dimension.

It is my wish that you benefit from my experience and are very successful in your own work. Nothing could make me happier!

1

THE BEGINNING

E VP (Electronic Voice Phenomenon) and DRV (Direct Radio Voices) are two aspects of the electronic oral communication with an unknown dimension of life where, as those who communicate tell us, the deceased go on living. They belong to the group of phenomena known as Instrumental Transcommunication (ITC).

Both EVP and DRV refer to audio communications, usually verbal but they can also be musical, with intelligent entities that contact people on the earth who work with this method.

Although I dislike the word phenomena to classify these amazing communications, I will use it to simplify the task of finding new words to describe them, thus reducing the risk of creating more confusion in an area already prone to misunderstandings.

True electronic contact with the deceased seems to have started almost simultaneously in Europe and the USA by the middle of the 20th century. But there were previous attempts to achieve electrical, and later electronic contact with the next dimension of life, apparently with success. I offered a comprehensive description of the first endeavours to contact the deceased through the new methods in other writings (e.g., Cardoso, 2010).

But it was the Swedish painter, film director and opera singer Friedrich Jürgenson who, with no knowledge of preceding events in this field, spread to the world the news of his own spontaneous electronic contacts with voices asserting to belong to the deceased. He is rightly called the great pioneer, the "father of the electronic voices". Subsequently, the Latvian scholar, Dr Konstantin Raudive, a former disciple of Jürgenson, initiated and implemented the scientific approach to these extraordinary voices. His book *Breakthrough* (1971) is, still today, one of the most meticulous and valuable works on the Electronic Voice Phenomenon or EVP. Others followed and we will talk about them throughout this work.

The DRV differ from the EVP voices in that they can be heard in the air, directly from the loudspeaker of a radio, and thus allow for short dialogues. In very exceptional cases, the dialogues are long, comprehensive and offer mindboggling information on the purpose of life and the living conditions in the next plane of existence. But, on the whole, DRV dialogues, although meaningful, are incipient. Not much more is necessary, however, to overwhelm with joy and hope the heart of someone who lost a dearly loved one. To give you an example, if a juvenile voice replies to her (or his) question during an ITC session, "May I speak with my beloved son Charlie?" something like "I'm very happy ma, I'm in heaven!" or "It's me ma, I live! I can see you!" directly from the radio, this is an unparalleled reward, a joy that will be with the bereaved parent, or whoever, forever: something that will never be forgotten. As a matter of fact, this is one of the main reasons, as our ITC communicators tell us, why scientists in the next world devised the new method of inter-dimensional communication.

EVP voices

I do not know who initially chose the acronym and the term to designate the anomalous electronic voices, but when the famous book by the great pioneer Dr Konstantin Raudive was translated and published in English with the title of *Breakthrough* (1971), it caused great furore, and many among the English speaking public started experimenting with the new method. Actually, this happening and the results obtained by the public in general were of such magnitude that these mysterious voices were soon to be called the "Raudive voices". I suppose this was the first or, at any rate, the popular designation for them.

Overall, EVP voices tell us that they are the deceased speaking from another world. They tell us that they transited to this new dimension after physical death. At the time of the electronic voices' pioneers, Friedrich Jürgenson and Konstantin Raudive, the voices appeared recorded on tapes; since then and until today, other recording media such as computers, digital recorders, video cameras, etc. were used with the same positive results.

Besides the EVP and the DRV, ITC comprises several other electronic manifestations, namely images and written messages digitally transmitted, as well as telephone calls and other electronic demonstrations with the same purpose, which clearly seems to be the confirmation of survival after bodily death.

But this handbook is about the verbal anomalous electronic communications, commonly known as EVP. We will primarily discuss these.

Apparently, the voices sound like human voices and the messages they convey are usually short; often, but not necessarily, they are mono or duo syllabic and may reply to questions, or thoughts, put forward by the person experimenting. Frequently they are feeble but, again, not always. Their main characteristic is that they can be heard only when the electronic medium where they have been recorded is rewound and played back.

Needless to say that in a country such as Great Britain, at the time so devoted to Spiritualism and the phenomena that revolve around it, forces averse to the new, 'revolutionary' electronic method, which in principle allows for direct contact with the deceased, immediately built up.

A good number of mediums and orthodox parapsychologists launched a campaign to harm the reputation of these extraordinary voices that tell us they "are the dead speaking from another world". This debasing movement spread to a huge English speaking country, the USA, causing a wave of discredit in this part of the world that lasted until today. Recently, the antagonism against the electronic contact with the next dimension of life seemed to start waning, particularly in the United Kingdom where it was predominant.

How do EVP voices happen?

Going back to the voices proper, these strange utterances appear on the recording device used by the experimenter on the earth trying to establish contact. Therefore, they are the outcome of a deliberate action to attempt the contact with an unknown dimension of life. However, it was not always so because, for example, Friedrich Jürgenson, 'the father of the voices', did not work for a contact with the next world; unforeseen voices appeared recorded on his tapes while he was carrying out different work, i.e., recording bird song for a documentary. The same thing happened with few others before him (see Cardoso 2010). However, in general, the voices do not appear spontaneously as some people seem to believe. I said 'in general' and this is exactly what I mean because sometimes, albeit less frequently, spontaneous anomalous recordings may occur.

The question of how the voices happen is a difficult one because, to this day, nobody has truly found out how they are produced. Many theories have been offered, principally by the highly knowledgeable Italian researcher Dr Engineer Carlo Trajna (see *ITC Journal* 1-7, 43, 44, 45). However, as we should expect, those were not experimentally confirmed as the sole explanation. Some of the voices happen as Dr Trajna posits but others do not. One important characteristic of the so-called paranormal is that although it is repeatable, it is certainly not repeatable on request. Any EVP/ITC experimenter should keep it in mind.

In this manual I will offer my readers what I deem most important for EVP beginners. This is not a technical book at all.

I am not a technician and my technical knowledge is very basic. Furthermore, I have no inclination to, or interest in, technical matters. To give you an example; I did not know how a computer worked when I started experimenting with EVP at the end of 1997! I had never had to use one in my professional work. And almost the same thing happened with audio recorders.

This is simply an unpretentious guide by an EVP and ITC operator who obtained results in her quest. I will point out to my readers what I found out throughout these years and will call their attention to little mistakes that we all do but which can be avoided, thus gaining precious time for the study and research of these baffling, beautiful voices. I urge everyone who reads this booklet to consider it solely for what it is - a modest and friendly gesture of support and cooperation towards all who endeavour to open the path to a new understanding of life and, ultimately, to a paradigm shift.

One last important advice is that although I will put forward procedures, which worked for me, they are by no means the only ones or the right ones. Each EVP operator and researcher should find the best way onwards in his or her experiments. And surely that will be the way, which fits best her or his sensitivity, mindset and preferences. The practices I suggest in this work are just general guidelines, which may help but will not guarantee that anomalous electronic voices are received.

2

EXPERIMENTING WITH EVP

Preparation for the Experiments

Not knowing how the anomalous electronic voices happen, but knowing that they do happen, we might wish to experiment with them. With this purpose in mind, I will outline what, in my opinion, are the main desirable conditions from the part of the experimenter on the earth.

Firstly, an attitude of seriousness and honesty is important. Secondly, a state of tranquillity of the mind is also advantageous. Anxiety is not a good companion in this field. Thirdly, perseverance because you need to keep at it even if you do not get results. We never know when, or if, they will come. But we must try for them. I suspect that true interest from our side is an inspiring and convincing incentive to our partners from another dimension. I always quote my first loud, clear voices, which said exactly this, "Contact!" when I asked what the main requisite for the establishment of communications with the next world was. And this advice was repeated several times in response to my questions, which were, basically, "How can I, from my side, contribute to the establishment of contacts with your world?" Thus, to strive for the contacts to happen seems to be a good way to open the doors to the mysterious unknown.

Moreover, in my opinion, the ideal approach to EVP (or ITC) experiments is a spontaneous, relaxed and optimistic attitude. If the voices happen, marvellous! But if they do not happen, we carry on with our life and continue to experiment for years on end, if we so wish, not allowing resentment or anxiety to take over.

And we reach the ultimate condition to try for our contacts – genuineness. Above all, just be yourself in this venture. A pure spirit, a clear mind and a generous heart are attributes that will help the work.

What to do when we decide to start our EVP experiments?

It is important to clarify that no ritual is necessary for our EVP work. I mean, you do not have to meditate or to pray, light candles, listen to soft music, be in the dark and so on. But if you feel comfortable doing any of these things or all of them, go ahead! They do not hurt. However, I believe they do not help, either, unless you feel an inner need to perform them, or any of them. It is a matter of personal preferences.

I have never carried out any special practices before my experiments. To tell the truth, I even feel a certain aversion towards these habits and rites, which give sceptics a motive, albeit unjustified, to disregard the attempts to contact the deceased and to consider them obscurantist and irrational practices. I have not performed any such rituals but I gladly acknowledge that, if deeply felt, simple, harmless rites might very well help the experiments because they may induce an open and receptive state of mind in the operator.

Therefore, do what you feel like doing but do it with respect and seriousness. This is my sole recommendation. Speak to our invisible communicators as you would speak to beloved visible partners, friends or family members. Remember that to get a reply across to you demands tremendous effort and work from their side, as they tell us repeatedly.

The place

You may try for the voices almost anywhere, outside or inside, if the place chosen is not noisy or chaotic. The location may be slightly noisy but, in that case, the noises should be controllable i.e., identifiable, otherwise you may think that you have recorded an EVP voice and it is nothing of the sort; it is just a noise (or a normal human voice) that you did not notice while recording.

Having said that, for my own experiments I prefer a small studio or a quiet room within my home. And the reason is that if noises occur during the experiment, they are more easily identified. This is the reason why I prefer to carry out my EVP sessions indoors. Noises are more difficult to control outside, unless you choose a very quiet place with no neighbours nearby, no wind blowing or heavy traffic noise, etc.

I have also tried to record outside, for instance on a solitary beach or by a river; in the woods, in the countryside and I did get results but it became definitely more difficult to be absolutely sure that the voices (which are normally faint at the beginning) were anomalous. It was the utterances' content that made me catalogue them as true EVP voices. However, to enable us to do this, the voices need to be clear and loud, and, although this may happen, it seldom happens when we start our EVP experiments. Good microphones have greater reach than the human ear and, therefore, it is impossible to be absolutely sure that what we recorded was not a normal voice uttered far away that we could not hear directly.

The log

For the purpose of identifying noises and for future guidance, it is very important to keep a log where you will register everything that happened during the 10 or 15 minutes of your recording session.

To start with, you should enter the name of the operator and participants, if they are present; the year and the day of the month, the hour and the atmospheric conditions. Secondly and most important, the location and all the noises that occurred while you experimented - from the slamming of a neighbour's door that echoed inside your house, to the dog barking or a motorbike on the street, the sound of a television set turned on in another room of the house, etc. Absolutely everything should be registered in the little diary, which you should keep for your EVP tests.

The state of mind and emotions of the experimenter and, if feasible, of the participants, should also be written down. Things such as how each one feels, e.g. tired, energetic or depressed, are interesting factors to take note of. You can experiment alone or with a small group of friends or family members. The important thing is that a relaxed, harmonious state of mind and atmosphere prevail among the members of the group, no matter who they are.

Besides the atmospheric conditions of the day and night of the experiment, the phases of the moon are interesting information to keep record of, also because, in time, it will allow you to have an idea of the most favourable conditions for your EVP experiments. For instance, it has been acknowledged by a majority of EVP and ITC operators that the waxing moon and the full moon are the most favourable for the voices to appear. And although we do not know the reasons for that, I corroborate the observation notwithstanding the fact that I have received voices in all phases of the moon. However, the ones pointed out above are certainly the most propitious, in particular for the EVP work.

Besides keeping a diary containing all possible information relevant to the experiment, at the beginning of each recording session you should also dictate loudly, so that the information will be recorded, the main important factors concerning the experiment, namely the place, the names of the people present, the date, the hour, the weather conditions and the phase of the moon. In addition, I normally insert a silent pause between each recording session. It will facilitate the listening and the cataloguing of the recordings later on.

The schedule

Before you start your EVP experiments, you should decide on a working calendar. Once or twice a week is sufficient. More than thrice a week is not advisable because it would either make you too tired or create the conditions for an obsession to develop. But, once you decide on an experimentation schedule, you should keep to it. From the psychological point of view, this commitment will be a sign of respect and affection towards our partners.

As any EVP experimenter knows from practice, the twilight hours are the most favourable time of the day for the experiments. This does not mean that you will not get results during other periods of the day or night, but the transition from the day to the evening seems to be a good time. Nevertheless, do not be deterred if you cannot fix a working schedule within these hours. Any hours are good if you are relaxed and emotionally available to experiment. I offer that the operator's state of mind is a relevant factor, albeit not a decisive one to determine the success, or otherwise, of the experiments.

Furthermore, it is important to perform our experiments at the same hour and on the same days of the week. According to the communicators, regularity allows them to track us down more easily. Once you start your EVP work, regularity and commitment are very important. Do not get easily discouraged and do not put other occupations ahead of your EVP work. Commit to it as faithfully as you would commit to anything of the highest value in your personal life. The attempt to contact the next level of existence is not a frivolous, eccentric or mundane venture. It is a highly serious project that can open unimaginable doors and change your whole life. Do it respectfully, with sincerity and enthusiasm. No secular privilege could be greater than being in contact with beings of another dimension.

As I pointed out above, at the beginning of my own experiments I used to ask my communicators repeatedly what was important for the contacts to take place. And, more than once, I received a straightforward reply: "It's contact proper". Thus, do not get discouraged and try for the contact with the next world with utmost seriousness, love and respect. My main recommendation is that you do it this way or do not even start the venture.

3

THE RECORDING EQUIPMENT

At this point, I am sure you are asking yourself what devices you should use. Basic and simple as it may seem, the truth is that all you need for your EVP work is a recorder and a microphone.

The devices are just the intermediaries for the voices to be registered but they do not influence the voices. However, the greater the quality of the equipment, the more sensitive, the easier it will be to capture faint voices and to be able to hear them.

But we need to be aware that much more important than the equipment is the operator's approach to the experiment and his or her inner disposition, as we have seen before. If you are willing to sacrifice time, social commitments and leisure opportunities to your EVP work, this will be more valuable than any other factor. We should keep in mind that our partners can perceive our thoughts, intentions and motivation clearly and, apparently, they attribute more value to those qualities than other conditions we may deem important. Thus, use what you have at home without spending unnecessary money. If you start getting EVP voices, then you can always acquire better devices.

The basic pieces of equipment you need for your EVP work are:

The recorder

You can use any recorder or a computer, too. The latter will be easier to work with because you will record directly on the hard disk and the playback and listening will be done at the computer, too. You will not lose time shifting from a recorder to a computer for careful playback and listening. But you need to have sound editing software in your computer because it will allow you to manage your recordings much more easily. As a matter of fact, basic sound editing software is practically indispensable for EVP work.

A computer is an extremely important piece of equipment to listen to our EVP recordings. As a rule, particularly at the beginning, we need to listen again and again to an audio clip where we found an inclusion, and this is more easily done with a computer. Also, sometimes we need to slow down the playback speed because the voices may be too fast for immediate understanding. In the old times, recorders had a slow down mechanism, which would allow us to reduce the speed in order to listen carefully to the tracks where we thought there was 'something'. But analogue recorders are no longer on sale, at any rate not in general. They need to be specially ordered. However, even if they were on sale, the advantages of a computer over a recorder are many.

Most of the old tape-recorders had a rotations counter, which is a useful tool for this work. Modern digital ones and computers allow you, easily and immediately, to mark the place on the track where you heard something or where you started and finished your EVP experiment, etc. You should certainly check that there is a counter in the device or the sound editing software you will use, but these days they all include that function - they provide the number of the track and the time in minutes and seconds, as well as a lot more information about your audio. Thus, unless you are going to use an old fashioned recorder, you need not worry about that.

A prevailing fallacy among EVP operators is that old-fashioned devices, valve radios and so on, are better for the EVP work. But this is not confirmed by the results or by the communicators. I reiterate that in the field of equipment, each one should use what he or she feels comfortable with. This is an important step to consolidate the desirable harmony between the operator and his or her equipment. And our communicators have insisted on this point as well.

The microphone

I know that a good microphone is expensive but here I would make an exception and recommend a good, sensitive, detachable microphone, if you can afford it. However, if you own a fairly good recorder it will include a not-so-bad built-in microphone and that will do, at least to start with. From my side, I have always preferred a detachable microphone because you can place it wherever you wish. I used to place it a couple of meters away from the source of background noise, i.e. the acoustic support (we'll speak about that in a little while).

The same recommendation applies to a recorder with a built-in microphone or to a computer (which, by the way, you can also use with an external microphone if you wish). Place the recorder, or the computer, between one and two metres away from the source of noise. The main reason for this is that if the noise is too near, and particularly if it is too loud, it will obliterate any possible anomalous inclusion. We must remember that we don't know how and where the voices are produced, thus, we must check every single detail in case it jeopardizes our EVP work.

Indeed very little, if anything, is known about the point of insertion of the anomalous voices. They are most likely produced in the microphone (even by electromagnetic interference) but we are not completely sure that it is so. Or maybe they are produced in the microphone but when a microphone is not available in the recording device, the communicators may produce the voices somewhere else in the recorder's circuits. In that case, we would not be dealing with a sound, which can be transformed into an electric signal only by the microphone, but with an electromagnetic wave, which would induce a signal into the recorder's circuitry. Such cases are very rare, though.

I am not suggesting that the electronic voices are 'aerial', i.e., that they are very faint sounds whispered near the microphone by invisible communicators, because we just do not know without a doubt how they are produced. At any rate, it is undeniable that when a high-quality, extremely sensitive microphone is available, the anomalous voices are not only of much higher quality but they are also more plentiful. And this could mean, for instance, that less sensitive microphones are not able to capture them (See Cardoso, 2012). Or maybe there are other explanations. Unfortunately we just do not know.

The type of microphone that EVP operators should choose is a topic frequently mentioned in the popular literature available to EVP beginners. However, I suggest that this is not such an important point, with the exception above mentioned. In the large sequence of tests we carried out at the Laboratory of Acoustics of the Faculty of Engineering at Vigo University, different types of microphones were used and they all recorded the voices, albeit with slightly different characteristics (Cardoso ibid, 2012).

It is often assumed that omnidirectional microphones must be used in EVP tests. Being aware of this information, I started my own experiences with an omnidirectional microphone: a Sennheiser. As the word implies, the omnidirectional microphone captures the sound from all directions. But the unidirectional microphones – designed to pick up their signals in one direction – which we used simultaneously with the omnidirectional microphones at Vigo University, also captured the EVP voices that were recorded (Cardoso ibid, 2012).

Moreover, there are the two well-known types of microphones – dynamic and condenser – but for our purpose that is irrelevant. Any one of them will do.

The sophisticated device set-ups

Readers deeply interested in ITC might wonder about the equipment used by famous transcommunicators such as Maggy and Jules Harsch-Fischbach or Adolf Homes, to mention two of the most paradigmatic ones who obtained the most amazing results ever. Indeed, some operators, and not only the ones above mentioned, use a combination of devices which, from our current viewpoint, do not make any sense in technical terms. I discussed this point with Professor Senkowski, the German physicist and one of the foremost authorities in ITC, and he fully confirmed this statement.

But the variety of those equipment arrangements is so great that I find it best to direct my readers to a good source where most of the 'classical' ones can be found. Besides, of course, Dr Raudive's book *Breakthrough* (1971), which, however, relates to Jürgenson's and his own time, primarily the 1960's, the latest devices set-ups can be found in Hildegard Schäfer's *Brücke Zwischen Diesseits und Jenseits, Theorie und Praxis der Transkommunikation* (1989).

A word of caution is necessary, though. Some of the equipment arrangements described in Ms. Schäfer's book, particularly the ones that yielded fantastic results, as is the case of the Luxembourg experimenters, Maggy and Jules Harsch-Fischbach, were devised and directed by the communicators. The same happened with George Meek and Bill O'Neil's famous Spiricom (Fuller, 1985).

To my knowledge, whenever such set-ups were duplicated, they did not produce significant results. At Adolf Homes' the high entities that communicated stated that between them – the ITC operator on the earth and his or her equipment – ought to exist perfect harmonization of [psychic] vibrations in order to achieve the inter-dimensional contacts (see Cardoso, 2017, pp 27-29). Perhaps this is the reason why the emulated schemes do not normally yield significant results. I believe this is the most likely motive.

Dear readers, as I normally tell people who ask my advice, do not imitate other EVP or ITC operators. Try to find your own way because surely that will be the best option.

4

THE BACKGROUND NOISE

I t has been amply proven that when a source of noise is available in the recording room or in the environment where the recordings take place, the quality of the voices increases. Basically, they are louder and more intelligible. This premise, which has been pragmatically tested and announced by several researchers from the beginning of the discipline, was experimentally confirmed at the strictly controlled tests described in 'A Two-Year Investigation of the Allegedly Anomalous Electronic Voices or EVP', which I had the privilege of directing (See Neuroquantology, Cardoso, 2012; Cardoso, 2017). Although not in such rigorously controlled conditions, which can be obtained only in professional high-level acoustic laboratories but, nevertheless, with the highest level of proficiency and great knowledge, the highly qualified Dr Eng. Carlo Trajna had already performed a great number of tests, which proved exactly the same thing (Trajna, 2012). And the many tests carried out by the Italian research group 'IL Laboratorio' on different occasions, yielded identical results (See Proceedings 2006, IL Laboratorio, the "SFINGE PROJECT").

EVP operators from all over the world use noise as 'acoustic background support' for their recordings, in the majority of cases, myself included, with good results. This does not mean that you cannot record without noise because you can: acoustic waves are everywhere – in the air and inside the device we use as a result of its functioning; nothing is really silent in the normal world. So, yes, you can record without a specific acoustic support but it will not be ideal.

Indeed, as it became obvious in the rigorous tests described above, the communicators use the noise existent in the environment to modulate their voices. This is one of the few conclusions we can put forward almost sixty years after the first electronic voices were obtained and understood as anomalous phenomena. And we should not forget that the communicators themselves advised Friedrich Jürgenson to "use the radio" in his experiments with the voices.

In any case I recommend that you use only controlled noise in your EVP experiments. As stated previously, the fact that it is controlled is of utmost importance. It will spare you the painful situation of finding out that what you thought was a message from a beloved deceased one was, instead, your next door neighbour speaking to her husband, or the TV set on in an adjoining room, etc.

But, worst of all is the effect it could cause on you – the inner conviction that you were indeed receiving messages from the Beyond. The subconscious plays many tricks on the mind and, if your expectations to get a contact with your loved one were high, you would never find out that it was your neighbour speaking, or the TV on in the next room, or whatever produced the 'voice' because you would take it for granted that you were receiving a contact. Your inner conviction would refuse the truth. This is a very dangerous situation and great care is necessary because wishful thinking and a normal human voice can cause much harm to a person's life. Please be aware of this possibility, which happens to a great number of people.

Having called your attention to this important point, we return to our subject, noise. Before we proceed, let me clarify that the simple fact that you record with noise as acoustic support does not guarantee that you will record anomalous voices. It will only help the voices to manifest but it will not make the voices happen.

There are many possibilities to introduce extra noise in a room. Whatever the noise, though, do not use an acoustic support that contains human voices. For instance, radio emissions in whatever language, or the novel 'Spirit Box' and, nowadays, the EchoVox, which has a database of phonemes, as well as the not so novel 'EVP maker' and so on.

They can all create confusion in your mind and may produce the same effect I described above, i.e. the conviction that the voices are anomalous while they are nothing of the sort.

Some years ago, a very popular method consisted of constantly turning the radio dial and recording while doing this. Fragments of radio emissions in whatever language were heard and recorded together with the operator's questions or comments. Some people would not even ask questions; they just recorded what the radio transmitted. Naturally, it was extremely easy to find pieces of speech, which seemed to be (or in fact were) in the operator's own language and which corresponded to the experimenter's questions, thoughts or wishes. The brain automatically attributes meaning to random human speech. This natural propensity of the brain intensifies under emotional stress, expectation etc. All caution is necessary!

The same rule applies to the 'Spirit Box', which, basically, is a radio scanner. And the same constraints I put forward apply to this method and to the EVP maker software, which uses chopped words. The program cuts recorded speech into pieces, which, subsequently are played back randomly and continuously.

But you may use a pre recorded disk or file with human voices. The important condition is to be able to compare after the recording session, if any extra voice came through. If you choose to use a pre-recorded acoustic support, the comparison is easy and unmistakable – any voice or sound that is not on the original pre-recorded tape, disk or file and can be heard on the material recorded at the EVP session, will in principle be anomalous; provided, of course, that environmental noises were fully controlled.

Be aware, however, that a few EVP operators have reported getting anomalous voices in the original pre-recorded acoustic support, also. I cannot offer my personal guidance on this matter because I have not experimented with it sufficiently. I used it once or twice during ITC seminars and, on those occasions, the anomalous voices appeared on the EVP recordings only.

Which noise to select?

At this point I am sure that many of my readers are wondering which kind of noise they should choose. Based on my personal experience, I will offer some suggestions about the noises that I find more convenient. But, to start with, let me say that all kinds of noise – provided it is neither too loud nor too low and do not contain human voices – are suitable. However, perhaps some are more appropriate for the voices' work than others. It seems that this is the case of radio noise.

Radio noise

From the beginning of my EVP experiments I preferred, and have used, radio noise as background acoustic support for my EVP recording sessions. And, later on, I found out that the fantastic ITC results of Maggy and Jules Harsch-Fischbach in Luxembourg, of Adolf Homes in Germany and Marcello Bacci in Italy, to cite the most outstanding ones, comprised amazing information transmitted by voices that, overall, came through radios. Although I never expected, or suspected, that I would one day be the recipient of the rare DRV, I thought that if those successful operators used radios in their experiments, there must have been a reason for it. Moreover, on the advice of their communicators, the great pioneers Jürgenson and Raudive had used radios, also so I kept to the radio noise.

Indeed, all successful well-known ITC operators used radios as a source of noise in their experiments and they all started by getting EVP voices. The DRV came later. This is the usual sequence of events in audio ITC. Later in this manual we will also discuss the DRV briefly.

Hence, a radio tuned in a point of the tuning scale where there are no normal radio emissions, is the ideal piece of equipment for your EVP work. The noise thus produced, albeit not identical, will be similar to the famous white noise, which in principle contains all frequencies.

At this point, many readers will ask: which are the most suitable frequencies for the ITC work? My communicators from Rio do Tempo Station replied to this question: "To modulate the waves we only need the short wave". And, therefore, from then on I tuned my radios in the short wave band. I was, however, already receiving the DRV and the communicators, as well as my question, related to those not to the EVP work. On the other hand, Friedrich Jürgenson and Dr Raudive, for instance, used the medium wave band.

In any case, radio waves in whatever frequency seem to be suitable for the voices. The important thing about radio noise or, as a matter of fact, any noise you may choose, is amplitude. As I said, it should be neither too loud nor too low. If it is too loud there is the possibility of not detecting the EVP voices if they appear. If it is too low the voices will be very faint, which is one more sign that the communicators use the extant noise to modulate their voices from it. Once, while experimenting with just a trickle of water from the tap as acoustic support during an EVP session, I asked my communicators if the conditions were right for their work and the faint reply which appeared recorded on the tape said: "There is not enough noise". Thus, noise of whatever kind should be kept at medium volume, neither too loud nor too low.

You can use one or several radios, as I do for my DRV work, but this is my personal choice. One radio is sufficient for the EVP work and also for the DRV work. However, at the time, I thought that if I offered the communicating entities a rich mixture of frequencies that would perhaps favour their labour, so I arranged for several radios in my studio to be tuned to different frequencies.

A personal choice

One important thing to keep in mind is that in this field, each operator should find his or her own way. And each one must choose what in his or her view would be helpful to the experiments. In a number of cases that I know of, personal choices are irrational from the perspective of our technical requirements or standards. Nevertheless, even if they do not make sense from our technical or scientific viewpoint, if the contact is achieved then they will be all right for the work.

On the other hand, I do not think any bizarre technical set-up we might put into place will be responsible for the success of the experiments if that is the case. We know that the success, or failure, of the experiments depends on an array of factors, many unknown to the communicators as well, as they have stated. But because we do not know what is truly decisive to achieve the contact, if we get results we should leave things as they are, even if they seem odd, and carry on with the work.

As I said, the communicators have clearly told me on different occasions that the "contact" proper, i.e. to try for the contact, is an important factor to establish and develop the communication with their world. Likewise, communicators from Timestream Station told Maggy and Jules Harsch-Fischbach without specifying, "So many things influence the contacts!" Thus, for the time being, I am afraid we cannot advance much farther in this field.

Radio emissions in a foreign language

Although I profoundly dislike this method on account of the listening delusions and inaccuracies it often generates, this is an acoustic support that many operators use and claim success with. I used it a couple of times only and had positive results at least in one of those. The method consists of using a radio emission in a foreign language, which does not resemble your actual language, as background acoustic support during your EVP experiment.

Upon listening to the recording, there may appear voices in the experimenter's language that did not belong to the radio emission. But, of course, this can be misleading because, acoustically speaking, there are words in a language which have a completely different meaning in another language even when the two idioms are very dissimilar e. g., Italian and Japanese. I have listened to several of such acoustic events in the recordings people send me asking for my opinion. Thus, I do not advise the use of radio emissions in whatever language and whatever way; a mistaken interpretation can cause much damage and create painful, false expectations regarding the contact with a beloved deceased one. Better to be on the safe side! We want real anomalous electronic voices, not ambiguous voices, which we deem anomalous...

However, if you are keen on using this method (apparently the anomalous voices are more easily obtained using human voices as acoustic support) there is a way to control the situation, as we have discussed above. A radio emission in a foreign language, ideally very distinct from your own language, can be previously recorded and then used as a source of background noise for the experiment. In ITC jargon those are called 'tin cans'. Upon listening to the recording, if you find words in your own language that clearly respond to you, they must be anomalous. Of course you should always compare your EVP recording to the previously recorded radio emission and be sure that the words or sentences you believe are anomalous are not there in the original recording. As I have posted above, there are reports of anomalous voices appearing in the 'tin cans' along with the radio emission used for the EVP recording proper and, therefore, those must have been produced by our invisible friends, also. But such cases are very rare and I don't think you need worry about it.

White noise generators and other possibilities

An alternative to the aforementioned sources of noise is a white noise generator. Digital ones have replaced the old electromagnetic apparatuses; hence, we need not speak about the latter. Currently any computer will generate white noise and also the so-called pink and brown noises. White noise comprises a wide range of audible frequencies. It is sharper and brighter than pink and brown noises, which emphasize the lower frequencies. Actually, these days you can find all kinds of noises in the Internet – orange noise, blue noise, rain noise and so on. Once again, it is a personal option but white noise would be my choice.

There is also the Psychofon, developed by the Austrian engineer and successful EVP researcher Franz Seidl, which became famous during Dr Raudive's time. Or the diode, introduced to Raudive in 1968 by Professor Alex Schneider, a Swiss physicist. The knowledgeable Theodor Rudolph, Engineer in High Frequency Techniques, also developed a Goniometer for Raudive's experiments. And these are only the best known devices used in the first years of our field of research. Certainly, several others have been devised by experimenters with a technical inclination but we do not even know about them. More modern equipment could also be suggested. For instance, the field generators employed by some operators, namely the German Hans Otto König who developed several different ones.

Nevertheless, be assured that none of those devices are truly necessary for your EVP work. The basic pieces of equipment you need are a recorder – these days practically only digital ones are available – or a computer to record with, and a detached microphone if your recording device does not possess an integrated one or if you prefer a detached microphone, as I do. I say that I prefer a separate microphone and indeed I do, but I have recorded voices with cheap battery-run recorders with an incorporated microphone. Again, it is a matter of personal choice.

Other acoustic supports you may use

Water noise

Some people like the idea of using running water as acoustic support. Water is beautiful and mystical and I think this is not a bad idea, but I never really obtained particularly good results with running water as supporting noise. I got some results but nothing to make me change my usual acoustic background support, which is radio noise.

What I said, above, about the volume of the radio noise applies to water noise, too. It should be kept at medium amplitude. Thus, if you choose a stream, the ocean, a cascade, running water from the tap etc., place your microphone at a reasonable distance from the water. And be aware of the wind. Whenever we record in a natural environment we need to pay attention to the wind, which very easily disturbs the recording, even if it is only a breeze. The wind effect on a microphone is highly undesirable and it will jeopardize the recording.

Traffic noise

You may be surprised by my mentioning traffic noise but it is, indeed, a good acoustic support, perhaps because it comprises a mix of frequencies. And, once more, the same rule applies. The noise should be of medium loudness. Thus, a house that is located near a busy street, albeit not too busy or it would mean unbearable noise, is suitable for your EVP sessions. The important condition, as always, is that no uncontrolled noises of human origin, i.e. voices, are mixed in it. Traffic buzz is suitable and, even if a motorbike is heard now and then, that will not disturb your recording.

Anomalous voices often appear 'glued' to a sharp noise. This happens with many acoustic supports and not only traffic noise. For instance when, together with a small group of friends, I started my EVP experiments, I bought a small kitchen clock to mark the two minutes pause after each question. A number of EVP voices appeared 'glued' to the sharp ringing tone made by the little clock. Interestingly, some of those were even within the ringing tone. We could hear the sharp noise and the voice simultaneously.

Music

Many people enquire about music's adequacy to EVP recordings. I thought the same and experimented with music, also. And I obtained results, although not particularly remarkable, maybe because it was a soft, melodious music with no strident tones. As mentioned above, the voices seem to benefit from occasional loud or screeching noises. Actually, at the beginning of the EVP work, sometimes even before the voices start coming through, as we saw above, blows and other knocking sounds may appear recorded. And, when the voices start, they may be preceded by two or three loud knocks, which were not produced in the recording environment.

We do not know why that happens or what their function is, but the truth is that anomalous voices will normally follow those bangs. In our Two-Year Investigation of the EVP Voices that I have been quoting, practically all voices were preceded by screeching noises, apparently introduced by the communicators, or occasionally generated by the devices. None were produced in the totally controlled environment where the recording sessions took place (see Cardoso, ibid, 2012).

Anyhow, music is certainly suitable for EVP work. But if it contains words it should be used 'tin-canned' (i.e. previously recorded, not directly transmitted) so that the original can be compared with the EVP recording in case the latter shows extra inclusions.

Rubbing a hard material

This method is frequently used by the people of the French Association 'Infinitude'. They record while scratching a metal plate with a cable jack or any other metal piece. The sound thus produced is sharp and the same principle that we have just discussed seems to apply here. They also write strongly with a pencil near the microphone, shred paper and so on. I have heard some of the anomalous utterances thus produced and the nature of the acoustic support visibly emerges from them. The fact that the communicators use the environmental noise to modulate their voices becomes even clearer.

I put forward all these examples with the purpose of calling my readers' attention to the fact that there are no limits to each one's creativity and that we should choose what appeals to us, thus adapting the experiment to our preferences and, in a way, making it more intimate. In my opinion this is a much better approach than copying other operators' models. In this area the importation of models, in opposition to what the great majority of beginners think, does not produce desirable results. As researcher Paolo Presi postulates in his book *Esplorando L'Invisible* (2012) "The experimenter is part of the experiment". I fully agree. Hence, dare do what you love, let your imagination fly and, if your communicators are able to get through, results will be forthcoming.

ADDENDUM TO CHAPTER 4

The broadband radio

Some twenty or so years ago it was quite common among EVP experimenters to use the so-called broadband modified radio to produce the background acoustic support used during the EVP tests. In 2001 I published a piece in the *ITC Journal* called 'Brief remarks on ITC: EVP experimentation'. It included a technical guide, provided by my friend Carlos Fernández, on how to modify a common, cheap radio to receive broadband signals. I reprint it below with renewed thanks to Carlos for his assistance.

Modifying a radio to receive broadband signals and function as a noise source[17]

Any radio that receives FM and AM wave bands can be modified to provide audio support for your attempt to receive EVP. It is not necessary that the radio be of good quality. A small portable will do. The modification is simple, and, with reasonable care, can easily be carried out by the layman.

Before starting work, if the radio is mains powered, it is vital to disconnect the radio from the electricity supply in order to

---

[17] Improved version of the text published in *ITC Journal* 8, December 2001, p. 16.

avoid any risk of electric shock. Do not reconnect to the mains supply until all the work is completed and the cover of the radio is correctly put back in place.

Step 1. Remove the cover of the radio, usually held in place by small screws.

Step 2. Cut the wire connecting the components board to the aerial. The aerial is then inoperative and can be discarded if you wish.

Step 3. Disconnect the variable capacitor responsible for tuning the radio. (For the layman, the variable capacitor in a modern radio is the small transparent plastic box, measuring approximately one and a half centimetres, which is connected to the other components of the tuning circuits). Cut this connection. As a result, the radio can no longer be tuned to any station, and if turned on would simply emit a continuous noise.

Step 4. To complete the modification, the tuning coil should be disabled. (To assist the layman, the tuning coil is a series of fabric-covered windings around a central core). Cut the wires connecting this coil to the component board, severing them as flush with the board as possible.

Step 5. Refit the cover of the radio, making sure that it is securely screwed back in place before you reconnect the set to the mains electricity supply.

The radio is now ready for use, and when turned on will emit a strong hiss of random noise (popularly called "white noise") in both the FM and the AM bands. This noise can be used on its own in your attempt to receive EVP or can be used in conjunction with any other source of random noise (usually a radio tuned between two stations). Make sure that your modified radio is placed at a safe distance from your microphone (approximately 2 metres). Adjust the volume of the radio appropriately, bearing in mind that for EVP you require only a moderate level of sound comparable with that received during normal listening.

5

THE EXPERIMENT

Frequency and duration

Recapping. Firstly you should decide upon your recording schedule. The best option is from one to three times a week. Whenever possible, you should experiment at the same hour and on the same days of the week. Also, preferably in the same place if you are doing it inside. As we have seen, the place you choose should be as much shielded from external noises as possible.

And now let's see about the experiment proper, starting by its duration. You may record for as long as you wish, but my advice is that you do it for no longer than 10 to 15 minutes. Besides the useless situation of recording for a very long time — longer recordings do not mean that you will obtain voices – the main reason for my recommendation is that the listening would be a painful, highly stressful job. Every EVP recording needs to be listened to carefully; and 10 minutes of recording can take one or more hours of your time if you do a proper listening. If you record for a very long time you risk not studying the file carefully enough and, therefore, you may miss a possible anomalous inclusion, normally soft at the beginning of the work.

I have already stated that no special initiation protocol is necessary for this work but, if you wish to invoke someone you love and with whom you would like to establish contact, by all means address that beloved deceased being. Think of that person with love, in tranquillity and in peace and request his or her help. Do the same if it is a beloved animal you would like to contact. Or say a prayer from the heart and try to keep inner peace. No matter how you choose to start your EVP session, do it in a spontaneous and heartfelt way. I emphasize that whatever you do in the field of EVP and ITC you should do it thoughtfully, with respect and with love.

The recording steps

I usually recommend that you ask questions to your invisible loved ones or, if you prefer, to the kind beings of another dimension who might be in the disposition of communicating with you. You need not have a deceased beloved one in the next world to carry out EVP work. You may wish to contact the next dimension of life because you are truly interested in finding out about the hidden, unknown aspects of existence or even if they exist. Whatever the reason, let it be truthful and open-minded.

I prefer asking questions to making comments or leaving an open microphone, as some people do, and request our friends to register their messages on the recording. The reason is that if clear replies to our questions are obtained, the evidence becomes much more convincing to us and to others.

Speaking about questions and replies, I will add that I often receive letters from people who tell me they experiment with EVP and get random words that make no sense. If those are real words (sometimes they are just hearing delusions), my advice is that you discard them. Random words are in all likelihood not anomalous and thus, not real EVPs. Nevertheless, I acknowledge that my statement, like everything else in this field, may be proven wrong. Indeed it is possible that one day you will record utterances that make no sense to you but will become relevant in the future. This can happen, although it is not very likely. The situation I described is one of the reasons why I much prefer an experiment with questions, because, in that case, any registered utterances should have some connection with the operator's question. Our communicators are intelligent beings and that intelligence is demonstrated through their replies.

In my opinion – and I emphasize again that what I say has no universal value for it is merely the result of a number of years of experience – the questions should be precise and require a short, clear-cut answer. One of the most negative features of our so difficult transcommunication work is unquestionably ambiguity, particularly when we make our own comments or questions. It is recommended that, at the beginning, the EVP novice should ask questions that require a monosyllabic reply. However, although I advocate short and simple questions that require short replies, I cannot fully endorse this recommendation. I believe it is a good suggestion but nothing should be taken as a 'bible creed' in our field. Thus, if your questions require a couple of words in reply it is all right. Open mindedness, imagination and audacity are good companions in our quest. Do not feel constrained by any rules especially the ones dictated by others.

ITC and EVP are 'forbidden' areas from the viewpoint of the current paradigm. We should not contribute to creating a behaviour paradigm inside an anti-paradigm! Hence, dear readers, take nothing for granted, do not try to emulate models but invent your own. Let them express your inner self. This is the way.

Going back to our recording session, we ask one question (or make a comment), we wait between one and two minutes in silence taking note of every single environmental noise produced in this lapse of time, and get into the next question. I say one to two minutes because, in my personal and other EVP workers' experience, this is the average time for a reply to come through. In fact, you will save listening time and effort if you keep it to a maximum of two minutes after each question. But I reiterate that it is up to you. If you do a long session, it will mean a much lengthier listening period and experience will tell you that this is not a good option.

Exactly because of the time required for a proper listening, five to six questions at each recording session will suffice. At the end of the experiment, it is good practice to thank our invisible communicators, just as we would do in regard to a human friend or group of people trying to get in touch with us, because, even if their voices did not get through, that is surely what our dear communicators endeavoured to achieve.

The questions

I receive many enquiries from people interested in starting the work asking, among other things, which type of questions they should ask and I usually reply that this is a personal choice. All questions are all right, provided that they come from the heart and you do not try to put our partners in the position of divination oracles, enquiring about frivolous matters or the future, something that would mean a tremendous lack of respect.

Some people also ask me how to make our communicators reply to them. Naturally, I cannot answer this question in a positive way because, as a matter of fact, we cannot make our communicators do anything. They do what they can and, I suppose, to a certain degree what they wish for but, above all, what they are allowed to do.

From the very beginning of ITC, this aspect of the contacts with our world, i.e. the necessary permission to establish them, has been emphasized over and over again. Oscar D'Argonnel, apparently the first person on earth to receive the anomalous telephone calls from the Beyond, already mentions his communicators' recurrent information that they "had not been allowed to contact" D'Argonnel on a certain occasion, or that such and such friends had not obtained the necessary permission to communicate, or that they "could not speak about such or such topic", etc. (see D'Argonnel, 1925).

As mentioned above, there are people who, instead of questions, make comments and leave the recording running.

And there are still other people who do not ask questions or comments and leave the recording running. (To my knowledge, this is the most unsuccessful method). I am a critical person and, as I said above, I prefer questions for the simple reason that, if consistent replies come through, they make good evidence. In any case, do whatever makes you feel at ease.

My last advice regarding the experiment is that you should not rush or be anxious. Do not expect anything, but trust life, the cosmos, God or whatever name you would like to use. 'Miracles' do happen! They happened to me and they can certainly happen to you.

6

THE LISTENING

A nd we reach the most complex stage of the EVP work – the listening. Listening to EVP recordings is a difficult job for various reasons. The first one is the indispensable concentration, without fail, on the recorded material. We should call it focused attention. This seems like a simple and obvious task but, as a matter of fact, it is not. And, while I write, a thought comes to my mind – if a sceptic reads these lines (an unlikely situation), he or she will be very happy and immediately think "of course it is a difficult job because there is nothing to listen to or to understand; it's all in their minds!" However, he or she will be wrong because to properly assess any recording – anomalous or not – he or she should be able to listen proficiently, and on the whole, people do not, sceptics included.

Besides words, there may be additional sounds in a recording to listen to. [18] The latter need to be taken note of carefully, also.

---

[18] The anomalous sounds need not be words. Knocks, the sound of a small ball jumping on a hard surface, and even whistles are rather common at the beginning of EVP experiments. No explanation for these has been put forward.

Because, often, if the operator does not concentrate on the listening, they will go unnoticed and the same may happen with the first faint word or words. However, let me make it clear that even in the case when a layperson does not hear a sound (or a word/s) because he or she lacks the necessary concentration or hearing proficiency, that extra sound or word will still be there, although almost imperceptible because the amplitude is so very low. However, no matter how faint, they exist and a sonogram would reveal them. This condition alone is enough to examine the recording with utmost attention and decide about the anomaly, or otherwise, of those extra sounds.

While I write these lines, it comes to my mind that the very first anomalous sound we received, when our little group started the EVP experiments, was a sigh. Not any sigh but a sigh of unusual acoustic characteristics, namely its proximity to the microphone while we were all placed a couple of metres away. As a matter of fact, not only did we keep total silence during our EVP sessions but the faintest noise produced in the environment, or involuntarily by any of us, such as a sneeze, coughing, etc. would be registered carefully in our log. This is an indispensable procedure if we want to do our EVP work properly, as we saw above.

Interestingly, sighs are common occurrences, in the initial EVP experiments of various operators, and a sigh is difficult to detect if we are not attentive enough.

Naturally, everything I put forward above is valid only if no normal sounds were accidentally produced (and recorded) during the experiment. The operator must be absolutely sure of this and, therefore, the log is important, as we discussed in a preceding chapter.

The danger of pareidolia

There is an important issue that should keep us vigilant when we leap into the adventure of attempting the electronic contact with the deceased. To listen to electronic recordings – often a mixture of noise and speech – is an extremely demanding job that needs the utmost concentration, particularly when the audio is not clear, something that may happen rather frequently as we have seen.

The main problem caused by the lack of clarity of a number of messages is the error they may induce in the experimenter's mind. Fatigue, expectation and the desire to understand what cannot be understood, may involuntarily encourage the operator to construct a full linguistic content of his or her recordings, which does not exist. Such imaginary messages may be publicized, as they often are, thus seriously adding to the damage already caused to the subject by sceptics and uninformed parapsychologists, amongst others. However, we should not forget that while there are innumerable situations of acoustic delusion, of erroneous linguistic interpretations of ITC recordings, which sometimes contain only noise, published in the Internet, others exist that contain clear, pertinent speech and information.

Moreover, the fact that any ITC operator may have both kinds of recordings throughout his or her experimentation is a reality that cannot be denied. Even in Luxembourg – and we should not forget that the ITC verbal contacts which took place there were the best ever registered in this world from the point of view of clarity – unintelligible voices also manifested, particularly at the beginning of the experiments. Maggy Harsch-Fischbach thoroughly describes the situation in her book co-authored with Theo Locher (See Harsch and Locher, 1995 or Locher and Harsch, 1992). But when the Technician and Swejen Salter came into the picture and directed the whole communication process, the voices became as clear as a good conversation with a friend here in our world. I have heard, and own, through the kindness of my dear friend Professor Ernst Senkowski, some of the Luxembourg recordings and can testify accordingly.

Going back to less renowned experiments, the problem arises when the ITC operator has insufficient self-criticism to recognize the deficiencies and indiscriminately publicizes both, i.e. fairly clear and totally unintelligible voices. The most dangerous situation, however, is when the operator himself or herself may be absolutely convinced that he hears what he tells others who, naturally, cannot hear it. Pareidolia is a psychological phenomenon in which the mind responds to a stimulus, usually an image or a sound, by perceiving a familiar pattern where none exists, e.g. in random data (https://en.wikipedia.org/wiki/Pareidolia). In our field, pareidolia can become painfully real and harmful. To keep the existence of this phenomenon in mind at all times is very important because it can save us much trouble.

Indeed, it is easy to imagine fantasies about voices that do not exist whereas only noise can be heard by anybody who listens to the recording. The most important factors that will induce delusions are, of course, wishful thinking, expectation and grief. Often the latter entails the former. A bereavement situation will very easily transform an accidental normal noise, which contains no words, into a message from a deceased loved one. I have heard many such examples. Please stay away from this situation at any cost! Keep your head cool and detached, even if the pain of bereavement is unbearable as it often is.

Back to our listening work

The track may be long – around 20 to 30 minutes if you have asked five or six questions – and total, continuous concentration for that entire time may seem to be an easy thing but it is not, because when I say total concentration I mean it. It is similar to the concentration displayed by an experienced meditator. I do not practise meditation but I have discussed the matter with several qualified people and I believe this is a good analogy.

Nothing apart from the sound should catch your attention. This is not only difficult but, if done properly, is also very tiring. When you listen to an EVP recording you should become one with the sound, and that demands full focused attention as we have seen. I mean, nothing else should exist for you during that lapse of time. It must be total absorption. But then this is a most difficult task because, without noticing it, your attention will move away from the sound after a few minutes, or even seconds, depending on the person. In consequence, you need practise but, in any case, do it for several short periods. For example, listen to two questions at a time and the corresponding periods you allowed for the replies. Rest for half an hour or a couple of hours, and continue. Do the listening when you feel fresh and relaxed and have not been listening to the radio, television, loud music, speaking on the 'phone, or talking with other people for a long time. We do not notice it but our ears, brain and the capacity for concentrated listening are disturbed, especially after speaking on the telephone.

The headphones

I no longer use headphones because I prefer to listen to the sound directly through the air and, these days, I usually receive the DRVs and not EVPs but, at the beginning, I bought a very good pair of headphones to listen to my recordings. Although expensive, this is a good choice if you intend to do your EVP work seriously, as you should. Moreover, the kind of headphones you should use is also an important point.

Personally, I do not like closed headphones because I feel that they usually distort the sound, even if slightly; so, I bought a semi-open pair of headphones. However, this is a personal preference. What you do need is very good quality headphones or, if you find them too costly, do without them. To wear a pair of bad headphones is worse than not using them at all. Bad ones will distort the sound, introduce echo and so on.

More tools that will help you with the listening

I mentioned the headphones but, particularly at the beginning, they are not enough. Even if not indispensable, it would be extremely helpful if you worked with a computer equipped with sound editing software because it greatly facilitates the listening.

We will contemplate digital recordings because, currently, analogue recorders are virtually unavailable and they offer no practical advantage over the digital ones; conversely, the opposite is true.

The most useful piece of equipment you may own for this work is undoubtedly a computer. The sound editing software will offer you many editing possibilities and, consequently, it will facilitate the correct interpretation of the voices. Furthermore, you can record with the computer proper instead of a digital recorder. It is more practical because your recording will be stored on your hard disk and you will be able to work on the sound files without having to transfer them from one device to the other.

One piece of good advice is that you listen to your recordings the next day and not on the same evening of your EVP session. As suggested, above, try to do it in the morning when your head is clearer. At the end of the day, our heads become saturated with sounds, including traffic noise, telephone calls, talking, television broadcasts and so on. Do the listening in the morning after a quiet and relaxed breakfast and I am sure you will perceive slight audio inclusions, if present, more easily.

Naturally, the use of the correct audio editing software for this work needs to be mastered but this is a job that can be learned. Like so many other things in life, it requires patience, practice, perseverance and critical sense. The other day, I found on the Internet the following comment about one of the most useful tools for our work, the noise reduction function. It was posted by an audio editing software company and it read; "Noise reduction, while clarifying the original message and revealing new ones, can also tend to change the pitch of the original voice and even alter the words of the original message beyond recognition. As long as the original clip is available for comparison, this will not be an issue since the reduction can be reapplied to achieve the necessary balance between clarity and the original intent of the message." Although this professional remark was not produced in the scope of the anomalous electronic voices, it is highly valuable information, which I frequently use in my own work.

In the next chapter, and with my dear friend Edgar Müller's[19] permission, I will reprint an excellent guide to the most useful software for our EVP work, formerly published in issue 52 of the *ITC Journal*.

Interpretation of EVP voices

This is a major point in our listening work and a tricky one, too. EVP voices have the advantage over other types of transcendental communications of being objective. A registered voice is a physical voice, which anyone can hear (and understand) at any time. Of course, this is true and of great importance but the prevailing problem is that a good number of EVP voices are feeble and sometimes muddled. In addition, typically at the beginning of your experiments, and often throughout your life, EVP voices will be no longer than four or five words or even less. Thus, if they are soft, often of very low amplitude, to listen to them and identify their meaning can be a painstaking and painful job. On the difficult task of listening to and understanding EVP voices, I recommend Alexander MacRae's book EVP and New Dimensions (2004). The author, a former NASA researcher, is a highly credentialed audio expert on human speech. He himself experimented with the EVP phenomenon and got positive results. His book is a real treasure of knowledge and rationality about our still mysterious field of interest and study.

Although the sound editing software will significantly help, it will not be sufficient to guarantee a clear-cut interpretation since much depends on the intelligibility of the original audio. The software will certainly help but it will not perform miracles!

---

[19] Edgar Müller is a knowledgeable Swedish EVP researcher and the *ITC Journal* Deputy Director.

Moreover, I reiterate that the software must be carefully used with proper knowledge of its functions and how they operate. If this does not occur, the software proper can introduce spurious elements into the audio file and significantly modify the recorded material. If incorrectly used, the software can dramatically change the timbre and the rhythm of the recorded word or words and, therefore, their interpretation.

Hence, your first task should be to study the software. There are two ways of doing this. One is through practice and it will take time. The other one is to seek the advice of a person who knows the software well and to work with her or him. Practice continues to be the key point of the matter but the guidance of a knowledgeable person will considerably reduce the time you need spend studying the subject.

Types of voices

We have been speaking of 'normal' anomalous electronic voices (pardon me for the contradiction!); I mean voices that are constructed in a normal way i.e., in the same way, or almost, of normal human speech. It is true that the grammar used by EVP voices is often odd but there are many EVP and ITC voices that follow the normal grammatical order found in common language. I am not speaking here of the anomalies that may be found in many EVP and ITC voices through electro-acoustic analyses. Those relate to the frequencies, rhythm, speed, modulation, etc. and are not perceptible to the layperson.

Besides the most common ones, i.e. the ones that are constructed like normal human speech, we may find several other types of voices in our EVP work. I will list the most frequent ones.

- Reversed voices; these are voices, which do not make any sense when we listen to them as originally recorded. But, when we use the audio software and reverse the file, they acquire meaning relevant to the operator and/or the situation. Although some people like to present them as characteristic of the EVPs, they are, nevertheless, rare. During all my years of ITC experimentation I received only a few of those.

One word of caution is necessary, however: unless the audio file, when reversed, becomes utterly clear and meaningful, do not take your recording for a true reversed EVP voice. As we have seen, those are rare and you might be fooling yourself by accepting a supposed meaning that does not exist and could even harm you (nothing is more harmful to an operator than to take a mistaken content for real). It is better to disregard those voices than to take them for what they are not and to 'understand' what they do not say.

- EVP voices in foreign languages are more common. It is said that the voices manifest in the languages known to the operator and not in languages he does not know. This may be true and Friedrich Jürgenson as well as Dr Raudive are paradigmatic examples of polyglot EVP recipients, but I have heard of a couple of cases in which the voices spoke in a language unknown to the operator. However, I did not study such cases and did not even listen to the voices concerned, thus, I refrain from making a definitive judgment about them. But if you master languages, you should be prepared for the possibility of receiving EVP voices in languages other than your own; not that it happens frequently, because it does not, but it may happen. I have a most beautiful example of this situation in my own EVP voices. I received several EVP voices that contain words in foreign languages but this one is not only the most beautiful but also the most emblematic. It says: "Natal, un beso for Nina" in a lovely, gentle masculine voice. Each word is in a different language and it happened when I was busy preparing the equipment for the EVP session. I had made no questions or even thought about any questions; I was just adjusting the recording devices. Thus, I could not understand immediately what it said, in spite of the fact that although soft, the voice is utterly clear. And this represents a good example of how the brain works in regard to speech of any kind. When the human brain needs to grasp the meaning of a sentence, the context plays a key role. It happens in any normal human conversation and also in ITC voices specially when the possibility of a dialogue, for instance in the DRV, exists. In addition, expectation based on emotional factors plays a significant role, often negative, in the comprehension of the EVP voices. We, ITC operators, should be constantly aware of it in order to avoid pareidolia.

Going back to my beautiful polyglot voice; "Natal" means Christmas in Portuguese, "un beso" is a kiss in Spanish, "for" is of course the English preposition and Nina was the name of my little female doggie Nina who used to be with me in the experimentation room. Besides, the voice happened in July not at Christmas time. As a result, "Christmas, a kiss for Nina" was only understood by me a couple of weeks later, most probably because I was not expecting this remark at all and certainly not in July! There was no context for its meaning. My beloved little dog's name, Nina, was the first word I understood after repeated listening and the one that led me to understand the full sentence.

I was alone in my studio (I cannot remember if on the occasion Nina was with me but she most likely was) and I had not yet started the EVP work. As I said, above, I was preparing the equipment for the session (the pertinent noises can be heard in the recording) and concentrating on doing that. I have wondered, many times, about the reasons why the masculine voice would say "Natal" in July. As always, we cannot be sure but maybe it was symbolic of the gift for Nina, i.e. a kiss! A truly beautiful EVP voice that I treasure. And I recall another occasion when one of the voices said in Portuguese "Doesn't Nina come here [today]?"

- Unfortunately, much more common are muddled voices, sometimes so muddled that we cannot understand them even using the software: noise cleaner, equalizers and so on. Sometimes syllables are so overlapped that comprehension becomes almost impossible. The 'time-stretch' function of the sound editing software will help but in the worst cases it is not enough.

- One characteristic that, in some cases, makes EVP voices more difficult to understand than normal human voices, even when they are clear and reasonably well articulated, is that the endings of the words are often whispered and barely audible. Perhaps the technical characteristics of the equipment contribute to this characteristic. However, at other times this does not happen. But, undoubtedly, the quality of the listening gear also influences our perception of the voices.

- As we know, consonants are decisive for speech recognition. However, sometimes consonants are softly pronounced in EVP words or missing altogether. But, as per everything I said previously, this is not definitive or general. Sometimes it happens while at others it does not.

One important final consideration: I have yet to find a parameter that applies to all EVP voices. They do not only vary from one operator to another but they also vary significantly within the same operator's repertoire. I am speaking of EVP voices, not of the DRVs whose characteristics seem to be more constant, at least in the scope of each operator's work. But, again, I request my readers to take everything I say not as the law or a rule but as a personalized example, which may or may not occur.

7

SOFTWARE FOR EVP WORK AND RESEARCH

(A guide for the beginner and the experienced)
Edgar Müller

The basic technical elements of hardware for EVP recordings have not been changed since Jürgenson's time. He used a microphone[20] to pick up the voices, tapes to store the recordings and a loudspeaker or headphones to listen to the playback. We are doing the same today but the equipment has, of course, undergone huge technical development, just like our telephones or television sets.

A main aim of EVP research has been, during the past decades, to improve the intelligibility of EVP. This can be achieved in different ways. For instance, to receive EVP having better phonetic quality either by using more efficient technical equipment here in our physical world or by getting messages of better quality from the entities sending from their dimension.

---

[20] In fact, we do not know what role the microphone has in EVP recordings.

Another method for better intelligibility is the improvement of the listening process itself, which is of particular importance, since most of the recorded EVPs are far from being clear and easy to understand.

And, in this context, there is a substantial difference between software resources of several decades ago and what is available today to practically anyone working with EVP. If Jürgenson, Raudive and their contemporary colleagues had the opportunity to observe us (which I do hope they can), they would certainly say something like "Oh dear, think if we could have done all that in our days…"

Via contact with people who send me recordings asking what I hear, I understand that there are quite a few who use Windows Media Player to listen to the recordings. The reason seems to be that they feel that software is too complicated. This is, however, not at all the case. Not using good software is a very strong limiting factor in the evaluation of EVP.

The available software can, broadly speaking, be divided into four categories, but the borderline between them is not crystal clear and, regarding functionality, there is a lot of overlap.

Audio Editing Programs, AEP, are in principle designed for handling music and they are very suitable for EVP work, even if most of them have many functions not needed for EVP. Needless to say that AEP are capable of recording as well. Some of them also offer tools for generating various sounds, like sine wave, white noise or ring signal.

Speech Analysing Programs are intended for phonetic research and they can be used in sophisticated EVP research as well, for instance to identify phonemes or formants and to get statistical data of recordings. The Speech Analyzer from SIL International is an excellent piece of software for such purposes. The Praat from the Phonetic Sciences University of Amsterdam can analyze, synthesize, and manipulate speech.

Programs in forensics; initially comparison of voices can be of great interest, also for EVP research. In this category there are also most efficient noise reduction software programs, designed to bring out human voices and to suppress surrounding noises, exactly what we need in EVP work. Unfortunately, they are extremely expensive.

Programs for medical applications are developed both for research and for clinical work, not only in the field of speech but also for the diagnosis of some diseases, for instance in MS (multiple sclerosis), where speech has an integrated role in the patient's symptoms.

Both program types, for forensics and medicine, have features needed for advanced EVP research but that topic is not within the scope of this article.

An AEP offers a number of most valuable tools for the experimenter or for the researcher, out of which the following are strongly recommended for simple daily work.

1. Incremental listening. Probably the most important and practical tool for EVP; meaning the ability to listen and re-listen to certain selected parts of a longer recording by moving cursors to different points of the waveform on the X-axis.

2. Changing the speed of the recordings is often necessary since such a function makes it possible to listen to the messages at a lower speed without influencing the pitch.

3. Noise reduction: if the recording is noisy this is often practical. However, it must be remembered that AEP are designed for music and reducing common disturbances such as hisses, clicks, pops and hum. A too-aggressive noise reduction of an EVP can, in fact, cause more damage than advantage in the intelligibility because important phonemes may be distorted.

4. Changing the amplitude, not only for the whole recording but also for selected parts, may be very practical.

5. To save certain selected cuts. This is, again, a very useful tool: to be able to save small parts of a longer recording.

6. Equalizers, Parametric filters and similar, to alter high or low frequencies; important tools due to hearing impairment in ages 60+.[21]
Additional to the above basic functions there are further options, such as:

7. Frequency and spectrum analysis, as well as phonetic data.

8. Changing file formats, bit rates and sample frequency.

9. To present two or more recordings on the same screen for visual comparison.

Some reasonably good AEP are available free, such as Acoustica basic edition, Audacity and WavePad free. These have more or less everything that an average EVP experimenter needs.

Others in this category are (approximate prices in EUR): Acoustica standard (35), WavePad Master (45), GoldWave (45),

---

[21] Presbyacusis, the impairment of hearing. Although most people are not aware of it, and are not inclined to admit it, the loss of hearing ability is a normal and progressive effect, starting already in late middle-age and increasing rapidly thereafter. In the beginning, only an Audiogram will show a decreased sensitivity of the ear and the impairment has no practical consequences; but from 60+ the loss of hearing may be noticeable in two ways: as a general reduction of the sensitivity and, particularly, the loss of sensitivity for the higher frequencies.

Sound Forge (depending on the version), AVS Audio Editor (55); they offer additional performance, which can satisfy the needs of EVP researchers working at a higher technical level.

WaveLab (88), Adobe Audition CC (18/month) and Diamond Cut (145) are in fact intended for professional studio work and, considering their price, it is doubtful if they can bring any reasonable advantages into EVP research. An older version of the Audition, v3 with full functionality can be downloaded for free. This one is, in fact, a slightly updated "good, old Cool Edit", which was a kind of the golden standard in EVP work before Adobe bought it, increased the price and named it Audition.

These AEP are to some extent similar, and to some extent different. Just like cars, phones, television sets of various brands, all have the same basic functions but differ in many properties, such as interface, ease of use, tools for editing, tools for recordings, layout of the screens, noise reduction, toolbars, work spaces and so on. None is best at everything and it may be a matter of individual taste which one an EVP experimenter may prefer. Several software programs are available as a trial version for a certain time or with limited functionality.

There is also a very simple, free AEP which should be mentioned, namely the WaveSurfer; this one is, however, too limited for EVP work and, in spite of the ease of use, I would not recommend it.

In my daily work I regularly use GoldWave, occasionally Acoustica standard, and moreover the Speech Analyser when needed.

However, my "fleet" of AEP consists also of Audacity, WavePad free, and Audition 3.0.

I have downloaded these, partly out of curiosity, and partly because it is worthwhile to know them a bit when communicating with colleagues who have them. Since I only use GoldWave regularly, I am not really in a position to judge the other software. Instead I render, here, some salient features from reviews found on the Internet, namely, "The Best Audio Editing Software of 2016". It must be emphasised that the AEP are tested and assessed as music editing programs and EVP work has, in several aspects, different requirements.

I add some of my own observations after having worked with them for a very short time, just to see what features they had.

Reviews of AEP

Audacity. My personal view: Clean and easy layout, many tools, for instance, 45 different effect possibilities, including change of speed and various filtering. Shows frequency spectrum but no spectrogram. An interesting feature is the following: when choosing to open a file the user is asked whether to open the original file or to create a copy of it and to open the copy.

The most common action we do when listening to EVP is moving the cursor to icons to start, stop and pause the re-play. In contrast with many other AEP, the Acoustica has a toolbar with large icons, approximately 10 mm on my screen, for these functions. It's a design, which deserves praise.

WavePad free. My personal view: Clean and easy layout; sufficient functionality for most purposes; has several filters; practical toolbar. Noise reduction is not the best. The free version has several limitations. Just like Audacity, the icons for re-play are reasonably large at the bottom to the left. In addition to all icons in a toolbar at the top of the screen, it is also possible to present a vertical box at the left showing all available functions in words.

Acoustica standard edition. There are three versions of this software: a free, a standard and a premium one. It provides very good presentation of spectrum analysis. This is one of the best and most affordable audio editors available; the layout and colour scheme of the interface are attractive and well-organized. The menu ribbon above the toolbar clearly divides the effects, plug-ins and recording tools into easily identifiable sections, which makes this audio editor easy to navigate. The audio restoration from this Acoustica audio editor is outstanding compared with the rest of the competition.

My personal view: For several functions there is a small round knob about 5 mm size with a tiny dot on it. The user has to move the cursor to the knob and turn it clockwise or anti-clockwise to change the values. This is a rather impractical solution compared with moving a mark on a straight vertical or horizontal bar.

GoldWave. GoldWave isn't the flashiest or most aesthetically pleasing audio editor but it has a large feature set, great file compatibility and tools to help you restore noisy analogue files to better quality. GoldWave's best tools are its noise reduction filter, parametric equalizer and click filter. The combination of the parametric equalizer and noise reduction filter lead to successful results in removing unwanted noise from recordings. This software is inexpensive and gives you professional tools to handle many different audio-editing jobs.

My personal view: A control panel can be opened and seen on the screen together with the waveform during listening and spectrum analysis can be observed simultaneously. This control panel is floating and its size and position can be changed. (See picture 1). ~There are practical large icons for starting, stopping and pausing the re-play.

SoundForge. This is Sony's basic AEP. Others in the Sony family are the Sound Forge Audio Studio 10 and the SoundForge Pro 11 up to 14, offering a much wider range of features. The interface is fully customizable and easy to navigate. There are several reasons to buy SoundForge including many digital effects, file conversion capabilities and a low price tag for an older version. One of the nicest things about using SoundForge is that the entire interface and the toolbars within it are fully customizable. In fact, this is one of the most customizable audio editing programs reviewed. You can change the arrangement and layout of the audio editing. This audio editor is loaded with a handful of effects and audio editing tools.

My personal view: A very attractive layout of the toolbars. Audio restoration (which means noise reduction) gives the user several alternatives to choose from with adjustable levels. The basic version is well suited for average EVP work.

AVS. The toolbar and ribbon provide easy navigation of the program and its tools. The audio restoration tools did not work as well as the tools in other programs. The layout of the interface is clean and logical. Each tool within your ribbon has a graphic with text to let you know what the tool does. These simple characteristics make the interface intuitive.

WavePad Master boasts a fully customizable user interface that both professionals and beginners will appreciate. The program took a long time to render to remove clicks and pops from our audio sample. WavePad has a clean and inviting layout. The tools within the toolbar change as you click on different tabs on the ribbon. This toolbar is helpful from an organizational standpoint. You can also create a customized toolbar to have any tool that you wish across the ribbon. Recording audio with WavePad is as easy. WavePad has virtually every effect and filter that we look for in audio editors.

Adobe Audition Creative Cloud is incredibly powerful. Not only does it have all of the functionality of an audio editing program, but also it has also the multitrack recording and editing capabilities that are associated with digital audio workstations (DAWs). The layout of the software is intuitive, clean and customizable, and the software provides an impressive toolset to handle any type of audio editing job.

My personal view regarding an older version (3.0), which I have: A practical detail is that when we mark a selection for listening, there is a small icon on the top and by moving the cursor on it up or down the amplification can be changed. The Equalizer has 10 frequencies ± 24 dB. Due to too many options EVP experimenters may find Audition overcomplicated.

Some practical aspects of using AEP

Are there any disadvantages regarding the use an AEP? The answer is only one that I have experienced, but one which can easily be avoided if the listener is aware of it. In the information technique the synergetic effect of audio-visual presentation is a well-established fact. In other words, if a speaker at a conference explains something only verbally the public may remember it, say, to a degree of 5. If the speaker only presents it on a projector without saying a word, a degree of remembering may be likewise 5. But if the public can both hear and read the message, the degree of remembering may be 7 - 8, much more than only via hearing or reading.

Using an AEP may lead to an opposite result because the intensive watching of the screen and, simultaneously, the listening, may split the concentration and the interpretation of the signal incoming to the brain. This is especially valid if the listener tries to understand, to interpret the waveform. My personal experience is that in rare, special cases when the EVP is very unclear, closing my eyes or not looking at the screen can improve the understanding.

It is common for EVP experimenters to use MP3 format when recording and sending files to others. This is all right most of the time, but it should be understood that the MP3 format was invented for music and is based on a destructive compressing technique, meaning that certain parts of the message are deleted or distorted. In case of reasonably good EVP this does not matter, but when handling an unclear, poorly articulated or noisy EVP, a WAV file could possibly make the intelligibility easier. A WAV file is not compressed and delivers the voices exactly as they were recorded. I always use WAV, it became a routine for me and the only tiny disadvantage is that a WAV file is approximately 2.5 – 3 times bigger, which in these days of high speed Internet communication and lots of space in the computers' hard disks is a negligible fact.

De-essing is a tool to reduce the excessive loudness of sibilant consonants, such as "s", "z" and "sh". These sounds can be annoying and disturbing in some recordings. There are various techniques to do this and some AEP has de-esser as standard, some others can be completed with plug-ins.

For good intelligibility, consonants have a decisive role as carriers of phonetic information elements, and this manifests in particular when listening to EVP voices, which are unclear, poorly articulated or have disturbing background noise. The consonants "th" "f" "s" "k" "t" have frequency characteristics reaching over 3000 Hz, and at over 3000 Hz the sensitivity of the ear is dramatically reduced due to age. The consequences are that elderly listeners do not hear the above consonants clearly or may totally misinterpret them. There is fortunately a simple solution.

Most sound editing programs used for listening to EVP have the option to change the sound characteristics. Therefore, elderly listeners of EVP may have the great benefit of increasing the higher frequencies in the program.

8

STORING YOUR EVP WORK

Cataloguing your audios

This is an important task because, if properly done, it will allow you to listen to your voices anytime you need or want to. It will also allow you to play them for colleagues or friends whenever you wish.

In case you are starting your experiments and have recorded a few voices only, remember that the number may grow and it will be a mess if, at a certain point, you find yourself digging without success for such or such recording. Thus, it is best to start cataloguing from the beginning.

I understand that each experimenter might want to choose his or her own way of classifying the voices. I opted for the date method, i.e., year, month and day for the simple reason that it is easily recognized by the computer and a computer is extremely useful for this work, as we have seen. Within each year I opened subfolders for the months, e.g. January is 01, February 02, etc. I named the recording proper with the full date followed by one or two of the most significant words of the EVP or DRV voice. The recording would then be 'saved as' in the corresponding date folder - year, month, day (by this order) and stored on the hard disk (or SSD) of your computer. If, with time, you record hundreds or thousands of anomalous voices, you will find this method very easy to manage.

As it happens with other important documents, it is a good idea to have a spare hard disk to store your EVP work as an automated backup copy. If something happens to your main hard disk, you will not lose your EVP files and will be very grateful for it. Alternatively, or additionally, you can copy them to CDs, DVDs or "memory sticks". It means more unnecessary work, though.

Another important step, if feasible, is to keep the anomalous recordings in the electronic medium where they were initially recorded. Obviously this renders the whole process more evidential. However, the possibility of carrying it out depends on which recording device you use. If you use a computer to record there is no problem, but if you use a digital recorder it depends on which kind because the plain ones have no great storage capacity and require information to be deleted in order to continue the work. Anyway, to digitise your recordings and store them properly is always a very important step in your EVP work.

9

THE DIRECT RADIO VOICES (DRV)

lthough this manual is about the basic principles to start experimenting with the EVP, I am sure that many of my readers will ask, "what about the Direct Radio Voices"? The truth is that there is not much to say about experimenting with the DRV, as opposed to EVP voices, because the procedure and the modus operandi are basically the same. The difference lies in the results and the results depend on our communicators. As I informed my readers above, I once asked my communicators on what the successful contacts with their world depended. Their straightforward reply was: "they depend on us".

Nevertheless, and understandably, each one of us would hope to receive the DRV. From our side, the only requisite for the DRV is the acoustic support used during our EVP session. It should be radio noise and not any other noise. As the name indicates, the Direct Radio Voices need a radio to come through. Personally I never expected to receive them but I used radio noise (the so-called white noise) from the beginning of my EVP experiments. Just in case... And to my great surprise, one day the DRV did happen!

My approach was basically neutral throughout the first two months of my EVP experiments, a period when I obtained no detectable voice results. I had knocks and what sounded like small balls jumping on a hard surface as I explained in another chapter but no voices, at least not the ones that can be detected by the human ear. And I certainly did not hope to obtain DRV because they were considered an extremely rare event in the history of ITC.

The protocol

The procedures, which I suggested in the previous chapters, apply to the DRV, also because the DRV normally occur in the course of an EVP session. In all the cases besides my own that I know of – Maggy and Jules Harsch-Fischbach, Marcello Bacci, Adolf Homes, Hans Otto König and others – the operators started receiving the DRV after some time experimenting with the EVP. This is what normally happens. Furthermore, the communicators of the well-known and highly advanced contacts, which happened at the Harsch-Fischbach's in Luxembourg, said about the famous 'bridge', apparently necessary for the most advanced communications: "This construction [of the non-material bridge] needs microphone recordings [EVP] on a regular basis by the human operators, with the purpose of facilitating the access to the human voice by the different groups of the Beyond" (Locher and Harsch, 1995, p. 143).

Yet, there may be exceptions, i.e. people who receive the DRV from the very beginning. But, in the couple of cases I am thinking of, which I know well, the truth is that those people had already obtained EVP voices before they received their first DRV but they could not detect them. They were so extremely feeble that they could not be heard easily; therefore, they did not know they existed. Nevertheless, as we should expect, when the DRV happened they could hear them directly. Several reasons account for this. Firstly, the DRV are normally louder than EVP voices; secondly, they usually consist of a chain of speech, which, however, at the beginning might be short. This is the wonder any ITC operator aims for and it does happen! Without prior notice, one day the voices will suddenly erupt from the radio loudspeaker and reply to the operator who had asked a question during her or his EVP session.

A wonder that happened to me against all odds. Atypically, my first DRV was long and very loud and it made me indescribably happy. I have told the story of Carlos de Almeida's first communication in my previous books, thus most of my readers must know about it.

People write to me and ask, "what should I do to make the communicators reply to me directly from the radio?" And invariably I answer back saying that there is not much he or she can do, except, perhaps, experiment over and over again (always without getting obsessed) with unbreakable patience. Furthermore, I am sure that a genuine attitude of hope and trust are positive factors that will contribute to the desired DRV contact.

But nothing can make the communicators speak by the DRV method if, for whatever reason or reasons, they cannot do it. As they say without specifying: "There are so many factors that facilitate the contacts!" Maggy Harsch-Fischbach states in her publications that she and her husband, as well as other participants in their experiments, got the impression that the communicating entities did not know exactly what made the contacts possible (Locher and Harsch, ibid, 1989, 1992, 1995). Thus, if the communicators do not know, how could we know?

I believe an array of factors merge to make the 'bridge' (as our transdimensional partners call the contact field) work on certain occasions (See Cardoso, 2017). ITC and EVP are highly complex means of communication, which do not follow our laws. But, to acknowledge this undeniable fact, should not make us give up our quest to find out the whys. Conversely, it should help us to accept that we cannot control the process, and that is certainly all right.

The shortwave band

I tune my radio receivers in the shortwave band in frequencies allocated to the State in the country where I live, the use of which is forbidden to normal people. This is a long story that you can check in *ITC Journal*s nº 41 and 42 and the reason why it happened was basically because I wanted to be sure that stray voices would not come into any of my radios. Moreover, many years ago, the communicators told me about the DRV, "To modulate the waves we only need the SW!" But it is also a personal choice because other ITC operators, starting by Jürgenson, used the medium wave band.

Anyhow, the MW is fine for EVP experiments but I believe the SW is more convenient for the communicators' work with the DRV. As I said, I use several radios tuned to different frequencies of the SW range. Again, a personal preference confirmed by my communicators. Actually, I cannot overemphasize how important it is that each EVP or ITC operator chooses his or her own method and, ideally, confirms it with his or her communicators. If that is not possible, follow your intuition for it is always the best choice. In addition, naturally enough, go for what yields the best results.

10

CONCLUSIONS

The nature of our work prevents me from offering my readers definitive conclusions. Rules and even criteria do not apply to this subject as I have repeatedly avowed. But, based on what we have discussed, I hope that each one will arrive at his or her own best methods. Please keep in mind that Rio do Tempo tells me repeatedly, "we are working to be able to speak with everyone in your world [who is] interested in our world [theirs]". What else could we wish for? Let us help them by striving for the contact earnestly and we will achieve it.

There are, however, certain guidelines that I may suggest, albeit with precaution because, as we have seen, nothing works as law in the field of EVP or ITC. In many cases the techniques may be similar but the results will differ. Does this allow us to think that the operator is responsible for the differences? Or, as some prefer to call it, that the 'mediumistic power' (even if we cannot define exactly what the expression means) of each one determines the results? I do not think so. That would be too simplistic a statement, which does not involve logical or knowledgeable reasoning. Moreover, we do not know what 'mediumistic gifts' in this context are; therefore, everything stays as it was, i.e., unexplained.

The truth is that, currently, we cannot identify the reasons why things happen or do not happen in our field of interest. It seems that unknown superior forces – and I am well aware that I am using a term devoid of content from the perspective of our actual level of understanding – do not wish us to know more. Naturally, I am just guessing but it is a theory as good as any other.

Therefore, from our side there is only one way: to do our best, work persistently and keep hope alive in our hearts. Many years ago, my communicators told me that my work was the best way to help them in their endeavour to speak with us. A few days ago they repeated the same advice. And, in the famous Luxembourg contacts, high entities from 'Zeitstrom Station' (Timestream Station) told us "a pure heart and spirit represent important beginnings for the contacts with our dimensions [theirs]" (Locher and Harsch, 1995, p. 148 French translation).

The main goal of this manual is to become a simple guide, although not a mandatory one, to all readers of good faith. I sincerely hope that it will help all those who would like "to know more".

It intends, also, to be a tribute to my beloved communicators who totally changed my life and made it immensely richer and meaningful. They contributed decisively to the painful work of broadening my perception of life and its attributes.

Finally, yet importantly, this book wishes to be a modest homage to the great pioneers who preceded us in this quest. My love and admiration for Friedrich Jürgenson and Konstantin Raudive are boundless and everlasting but others, deceased and alive alike, are also in my mind. They opened the way to me and to many others who will follow the same path. Hopefully, the current paradigm will finally be reversed by our joint efforts.

REFERENCES

Aimone Querio, L. Dalla loro parte. (self published, n/date).

Alvisi, G. (1976). Le Voci dei Viventi di Ieri. Comunicazioni elettromagnetiche con l'aldilà. Milano : Sugarco Edizioni S.r.l.

Portuguese translation : As Vozes dos Vivos de Ontem. Mem Martins, Portugal: Publicações Europa-América.

Alvisi, G. (1983). Dimensione Radiosa. Milano: SugarCo. Edizioni s.r.l.

Bacci, M. (1991). Il Mistero delle Voci dall' Aldillà. 2nd edition. Roma: Ed. Mediterranee.

Barušs, I. Electronic Voices: Contact with Another Dimension? by Anabela Cardoso. O Books, 2010. 236 pp. $24.95 (paperback). ISBN 9781846943638. Journal of Scientific Exploration, Vol. 25, Number 3, pp. 600-604.

Belline, M. (1972). La Troisième Oreille, Paris: Ed. Robert Laffont.

Belline, M. (1978). Anthologie de l'au-delà, Paris, Robert Laffont.

Bender, H. (2011). On the Analysis of Exceptional Voice Phenomena on Tapes. Pilot studies on the 'recordings' of Friedrich Jürgenson. *ITC Journal* 40, 2011, pp. 61-78.

Bender, H. (1970). Zur Analyse außergewöhnlicher Stimmphänomene auf Tonband – Erkundungsexperimente über die "Einspielungen" von Friedrich Jürgenson. Zeitschrift für Parapsychologie und Grenzgebiete der Psychologie, Year 12, Nr. 4, pp. 226 – 238.

Bose, J. (1902). Response in the Living and Non-Living. New York: Longmans Green.

Bose, Sir J.C. (1913). Researches on irritability of plants. New York: Longmans, Green, and Co.

Bose, Sir J. C. (1926). The Nervous Mechanism of Plants. New York: Longmans Green.

Bozzano, E. (1941). Popoli Primitivi e manifestazioni supernormali. Verona: Edizioni L'Albero.

Brune, F. (1993). Les Morts nous Parlent. Paris: Ed. du Félin, Philippe Lebaud (1st Ed. 1988).

Brune, F. (2005, 2006). Les Morts nous Parlent. (3rd. Ed.) Tome 1 (2005), Tome 2 (2006). Paris: Oxus Editions.

Brune, F. and Chauvin, R. (2003). À L'Écoute de L'Au-Delà. 2nd. Ed. Paris: Oxus.

Bruno, G. (1584). De la Causa, Principio e Uno.

Bruno, G. (1584). Spaccio de la bestia trionfante.

Capitani, L. and Pagnotta, S. (1990). Terre Tuttora Inviolate. Roma: Ed. Mediterranee.

Cardoso, A. (2010). Electronic Voices, Contact with Another Dimension? UK: Ropley, Hants, John Hunt/O-Books.

Cardoso, A. (2012). A Two-Year Investigation of the Allegedly Anomalous Electronic Voices or EVP. Neuroquantology, Volume 10, Issue 3, pp. 492-514.

Cardoso, A. (2017). Electronic Contact with the Dead, What Do the Voices Tell us? UK: Hove: White Crow Books.

Cardoso, A. *ITC Journal*, 2000-2017, Editorials. www.itcjournal. org.

D'Argonnel, O. (1925). Vozes do Além pelo Telefone, novo e admirável systema de communicação (Voices from the Beyond, new and admirable system of communication). Rio de Janeiro: Pap. Typ. Marques, Araújo & C.

Darwin, Charles (1958), Barlow, Nora (ed.), The Autobiography of Charles Darwin 1809–1882. With the original omissions restored. Edited and with appendix and notes by his granddaughter Nora Barlow, London: Collins, retrieved 4 November 2008.

Ellis, D. J. (1978) The Mediumship of the Tape Recorder. UK: The Author.

Fernández, C. (1995). Parapsicología Electrónica. Madrid: Ediciones Contrastes, S. A.

Fernández, C. (2006). Voces del Más Allá. ¿Hablan los Fallecidos a través de los Equipos Electrónicos? Madrid: Editorial Edaf S. A.

(El Archivo del Misterio de Iker Jiménez).

Fontana, D. (2005). Is There an Afterlife? Ropley, Hants, UK: John Hunt/O Books.

Fukuoka, M. (1987). The Road back to Nature. Tokyo, New York: Japan Publications, Inc.

Fuller, J. G. (1985). The Ghost of 29 Megacycles. London: Souvenir Press Ltd.

Grandsire, J. M. (1998). La Transcommunication. Agnières: JMG éditions.

Harrison, Tom (2008). Life after Death: Living Proof, York, England: SNPP.

Huxley, T. H. (1870). Lay Sermons, Addresses and Reviews. London: MacMillan and Co.

The Radioelectric frequencies of Rio do Tempo. The forbidden emission. (2011). *ITC Journal* 41, pp. 77-88; Part 2: *ITC Journal* 42, pp. 29-43.

Harsch and Locher. (1995). French translation : Les Contacts vers l'Au-Delà à l'Aide de Moyens Techniques Existent ! Agnières : Parasciences.

Jürgenson, F. (1964). Röstema från Rymden (Voices from the Space). Stockholm: Saxon & Lindströms.

Jürgenson, F. (1967). Sprechfunk mit Verstorbenen (Freiburg im Br.: Verlag Hermann Bauer. Republished 1981 by Goldmann Verlag (München).

Jürgenson, F. (1968). Radio och Mikrofonkontakt med de döda. (Radio and microphone contacts with the dead) Uppsala: Nybloms.

Jürgenson, F. (2004). Voice Transmissions with the Deceased. Stockholm: Firework Edition N° 101. The Jürgenson Foundation: http://www.fargfabriken.se/fjf/

Locher and Harsch (1989). Original German edition. Jenseitskontakte Mit Technischen Mitteln Gibt es! Luxembourg: C.E.T.L.

Locher, T. and Harsch, M. (1992). Transcomunicação. São Paulo: Editora Pensamento. (Portuguese Ed.).

Mancuso, S. and Viola, A. (2013). Brilliant Green: The Surprising History and Science of Plant Intelligence. Washington D. C.: Island Press.

Moreau, L. (2012). 6 « coups de fil » de l'au-delà. Le Messager, 78, pp.14-15.

Pagnotta, S. (1992). Risveglio alla Vita. Roma: Edizioni Mediterranee.

Raudive, K. (1968). Unhörbares Wird Hörbar – Auf den Spuren Einer Geisterwelt. Remagen: Reichl.

Raudive, K. (1971). Breakthrough: An Amazing Experiment in Electronic Communication with the Dead. Gerrards Cross, England: Colin Smythe.

Schäfer, H. (1989). Brücke Zwischen Diesseits und Jenseits. Freiburg: Verlag Hermann Bauer KG.

Schäfer, H. (1993). Ponte entre o Aqui e o Além – Teoria e Prática da Transcomunicação. São Paulo, Editora Pensamento (Portuguese translation of the above mentioned work).

Schäfer, H. (1992). Théorie et Pratique de la Transcommunication. Paris: Éd. Robert Laffont.

Scott Rogo, D. and Bayless, R. (1979). Phone Calls from the Dead. Englewood Cliffs, New Jersey: Prentice-Hall.

Senkowski, E. (1999). Transkommunikation: Transinformationen Rivenich 1988-1997 (Compilation of Adolf Homes' Messages). Vol. IV.

Senkowski, E. (1999). Transcomunicazione. Numero Speciale. Available from Dr Carla Castagnini, Strada Statale Romana Nord, n° 135, I -41010 Fossoli di Carpi (MO), Italia.

Simonet, M. (1991). Images et messages de l'au-delà. Editions du Rocher.

Simonet, M. (2001). A l'écoute de l'invisible. Enregistrement des voix de l'au-delà, images vidéo du monde parallèle. Editions F. Lanore.

Simonet, M. (1993). Porte ouverte sur l'éternité : L'Au-delà nous parle. Editions du Rocher.

Stead, W. (1922). The Blue Island. Internet Archive BookReader.

Théry, P. (2000). First telephone contact in France by Konstantin Raudive. *ITC Journal*, 2, 42-43.

Cardoso, A. (2010). *Electronic Voices, Contact with Another Dimension?* Ropley, Hants, UK: John Hunt/O-Books.

Cardoso, A. (2012). A Two-Year Investigation of the Allegedly Anomalous Electronic Voices or EVP. *NeuroQuantology* | September 2012| Volume 10, Issue 3, pp. 492 -514.

Cardoso, A. (2017). *Electronic Contact with the Dead, What Do the Voices Tell Us?* Hove, UK: White Crow Books.

D'Argonnel, O. (1925). *Vozes do Além pelo Telefone.* Rio de Janeiro: Pap. Typ. Marques, Araújo & C.

Fuller, J. G. (1985). *The Ghost of 29 Megacycles.* London: Souvenir Press Ltd.

Jürgenson, F. (2004). *Voice Transmissions with the Deceased.* Stockholm: Firework Edition Nº 101. The Jürgenson Foundation: http://www.fargfabriken.se/fjf/

Locher T. and Harsch M. (1989). *Jenseitskontakte Mit Technischen Mitteln Gibt es!*

Harsch, M. and Locher, T. (1995). *Les Contacts vers l'Au-delà à l'aide de moyens techniques existent!* Association Suisse de Parapsychologie et Cercle d'Etudes sur la Transcommunication du Luxembourg (original German ed. 1989; French Ed. 1995, Agnières: Parasciences).

Locher, T. and Harsch, M. (1992). *Transcomunicacão.* Sao Paulo: Editora Pensamento (Portuguese Ed).

MacRae, A. (2004). *EVP and New Dimensions.* Sanctuary Press; Lulu.com

Presi, P. (2012). *Esplorando L'Invisibile.* Udine: Edizione Segno.

Raudive, K. (1971). *Breakthrough: An Amazing Experiment in Electronic Communication with the Dead.* Gerrards Cross, England: Colin Smythe.

Schäfer H. (1989). *Brücke Zwischen Diesseits und Jenseits, Theorie und Praxis der Transkommunikation.* Freiburg: Verlag Hermann Bauer KG.

Senkowski, E. (1995). *Instrumentelle Transkommunikation* (first Ed. 1989). Frankfurt: R. G. Fischer.

"SFINGE" PROJECT (2006) *Proceedings.* IL Laboratorio Interdisciplinare di Ricerca Biopsicocibernetica, Bologna, Italy.

Trajna. C. (2000). The Psychotemporal Model. *ITC Journal* 1-7.

Trajna. C. (2012). Stimulated Psychophony. *ITC Journal* 43, pp 32- 43; Stimulated Psychophony 2. *ITC Journal* 44-45, pp. 87-113.

Lightning Source UK Ltd.
Milton Keynes UK
UKHW011945140621
385503UK00001B/111